Tales of the Old
COUNTRY
FARMERS

Daniel Orpin (with his head between the pegs), assisted by Jessie Clayton, demonstrates the use of the bar at the rear of this eighteenth-century mill. The steps hook onto the bar and the men push on the base, thereby turning the sails into the wind. This photograph was taken in the early 1950s

TALES OF THE OLD

COUNTRY FARMERS

Tom Quinn

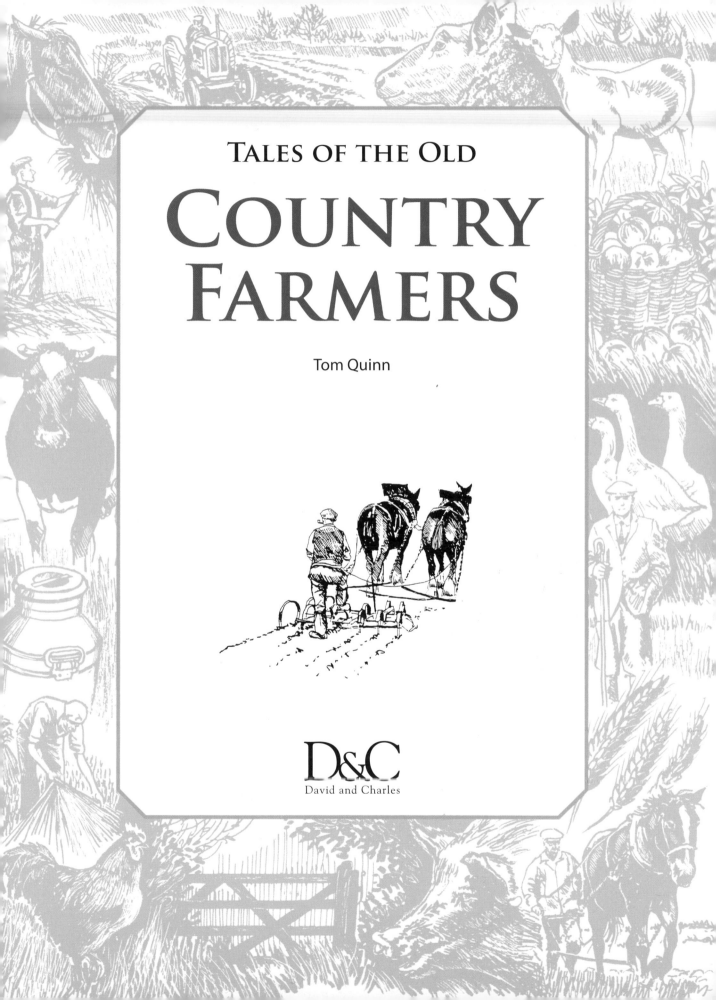

D&C

David and Charles

ACKNOWLEDGEMENTS

I owe an enormous debt of gratitude to the ten farmers whose memories lie at the heart of this book. All put up cheerfully with my endless demands for more information and with my limitless capacity to drink tea.

A complex illustrated book like this actually has very little to do with the author once the typescript has left his hands, but that is the moment at which a number of other people – particularly editors and illustrators – have to sort out the business of words and pictures and knitting them together. With that in mind I would like to thank Philip Murphy, who drew the pictures, and Sue Hall and Anne Plume at David & Charles.

I would also like to thank the following individuals and institutions: Harry Robson, J.T. Lovett-Turner, Arthur Court, E. Peter Day, David Powell, Mr Avery, George Pemberley, Mr and Mrs P. Quinn, May Constance, Mrs M.I. Greenway, John Williams-Davies, J.R. Hughes, Gerald Pendry, T. Erwyd Howells, Robin Belben, J.A. Tomkins, H. Oswald Harrison, George Gadwell Hall, Mr and Mrs A.J.T. Guest, Karen Warren of Pipe Dreams, Sarah Storey, Barbara Thompson, S.J. Guest, Debbie Fischer, Miss L. Plummer, Mary Corbett, Corinna Button, Simon Marshall, The British Library, The National Farmers Union and The Time Machine.

PHOTOGRAPH ACKNOWLEDGEMENTS

The author and publishers would like to thank the following individuals and organisations for supplying photographs: The 'Topical' Press Agency Ltd (p2); Ronald Goodearl (p8); Fox Photos Ltd (pp10, 32, 101, 104, 108–9); Reuter Photos Ltd (p33); John A. Pearce (p40); John Tarlton (pp44, 48, 49, 56, 60, 61, 134, 168); St John's Photography (p52); G.S. McCann (pp117, 118, 124, 126); Associated Photo Services (p120); Bertram Unne (p121); Grove Studios (p141). Every effort has been made to trace copyright holders of all the photographs, but if any have been missed we apologise.

A DAVID & CHARLES BOOK
David & Charles is a subsidiary of F+W (UK) Ltd.,
an F+W Publications Inc. company

First published in the UK in 1995
Reprinted 1995 (three times), 1996, 2005
First paperback edition 2006

Text copyright © Tom Quinn 1995, 2006

Tom Quinn has asserted his right to be identified as author of this work in accordance with the Copyright, Designs and Patents Act, 1988.

A catalogue record for this book is available from the British Library.

ISBN 0 7153 0154 3 hardback
ISBN 0 7153 2418 7 paperback

Typeset by ABM Typographics Ltd, Hull
Printed in United Kingdom by Butler & Tanner Ltd
for David & Charles
Brunel House   Newton Abbot   Devon

Visit our website at www.davidandcharles.co.uk

David & Charles books are available from all good bookshops; alternatively you can contact our Orderline on 0870 9908222 or write to us at FREEPOST EX2 110, D&C Direct, Newton Abbot, TQ12 4ZZ (no stamp required UK mainland); US customers call 800-289-0963 and Canadian customers call 800-840-5220.

CONTENTS

Introduction   9

Quoits and Carters · *Will Constance, Scole, Norfolk*   11

High Days and Holidays · *Reg Dobson, Newton, Warwickshire*   27

'The World's All Wrong' · *Joe White, Chagford, Devon*   47

The Musician of the Fields · *Lance Whitehead, Tenterden, Kent*   63

A Marshman, Born and Bred · *Richard Body, Romney Marsh, Kent*   83

A Boy at the Plough · *William Wade, Longnewton, Cleveland*   99

A Farming Dynasty · *Dick Rowley Williams, Denbigh, North Wales*   115

At the Hiring Fair · *John Elgey, Great Driffield, Humberside*   131

Button Hooks and Britches · *Aubrey Charman, Horsham, Sussex*   147

Shepherd and Horseman · *George Greenheld, Bilborough,
   North Yorkshire*   167

Index   181

INTRODUCTION

A time-traveller from the Middle Ages wandering the fields of England during the first three decades of this century would have been astonished at the great, laborious steam engines that helped with the harvest in many areas; but in almost every other respect he would have recognised immediately agricultural practices and traditions little changed since the close of the Dark Ages. Horses had replaced oxen, it is true, and the great fields divided into strips had gone, but the countryside was still a place where mechanisation had made only minor inroads. The steady pace of life was dictated by the horse; animals were driven to market along the ancient drovers' roads, and tiny fields surrounded by well-grown hedges dominated much of the landscape.

At the beginning of this century the countryside was a much more densely populated place than it is today: a lowland farmer might employ a shepherd, a team of horsemen and their assistants, a cowman, milkmaids and odd-job men. All had tied cottages, and although they often lived at or beneath the poverty line, they had sufficient finances to fuel a local economy of shops, pubs, blacksmiths, wheelwrights and farriers, which now has all but disappeared.

Our medieval time-traveller would also have recognised the local nature of life in a society where few people travelled anywhere outside their immediate environment, and if they did travel at all, it was on foot. In the pubs, clay pipes were still smoked beneath the gloomy light thrown by candles and oil lamps, and the dust rose in summer from the winding, unmade roads.

It was World War II that accelerated a process of change in the countryside that had begun in the Great War. Change had to come because, at a time of national crisis, it was essential that farmers should use the latest chemicals and technology in order to produce the maximum amount of food. After that there was no going back.

With the advent of the mass-produced motor car, tractors and combine harvesters, and also the development of chemical fertilisers, the last great movement from the land to the towns and cities took place. The heavy horses that had powered the farming world for so long vanished within a few years, along with most of the farmworkers' jobs, and by the late 1950s and early 1960s, many villages had become mere dormitories for the towns; men who might once have worked on the land now drove away from the village each day to work in factories and offices. Today our medieval time-traveller would find himself lost in an unfamiliar world, a rural world so dominated by tractor and car that it more nearly reflects the values of the town.

The old values and way of life may have entirely vanished, but many of the men who knew that horse-driven world at first-hand are still alive, though now in their eighties and nineties. And it is their memories of a vanished world – a world that links us directly to our

Heading for home: a summer afternoon in Hertfordshire towards the end of the 1930s

A mobile shop's tour of rural Oxfordshire in the mid-1950s ends in Burford

medieval ancestors – that are recorded here. Moreover their recollections of this world have a particular value, because although they record some of the most attractive aspects of an essentially pre-industrial English countryside, they also include memories of hardship and deprivation, and are therefore recollections that should act as a caution to those who over-idealise the rustic past.

The farmers who agreed to talk to me include men who come from widely differing social backgrounds; at one extreme there is the gentleman farmer who inherited everything, and at the other the labourer who scraped together enough money at last to take a lease on his own farm.

Most of us have an image of the countryside which is based on nostalgia for some rustic ideal; but if this book has any merit at all it lies in the fact that it re-creates the past as far as possible *as it was*, and not as we might have liked it to be. Nevertheless, for all its realism, this portrait of the past is, I hope, both a tribute to those who once worked the land and an attempt to preserve the best of it from the long oblivion of history.

TOM QUINN – 1994

QUOITS AND CARTERS

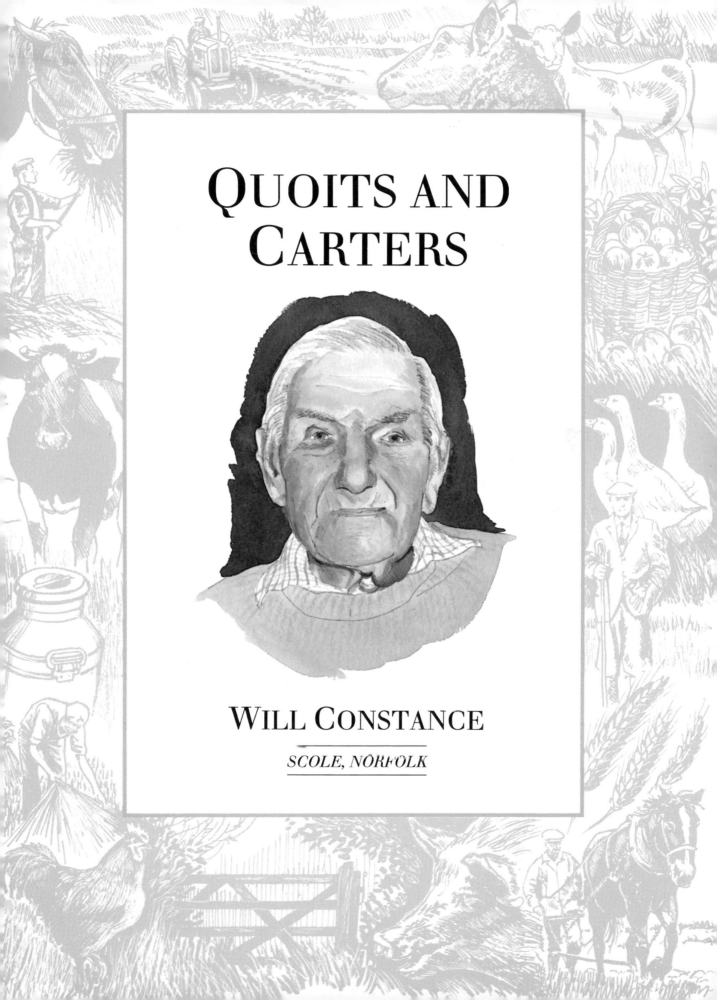

WILL CONSTANCE

SCOLE, NORFOLK

'Villages were still served by delivery vans pulled by horses'

Will Constance is ninety-two and has spent his life in one of the most traditionally agricultural parts of the country: Norfolk. Until the building of the M11, Norfolk, like most of East Anglia, was cut off from the main north–south road and rail routes which brought change and development to other parts of the country. In the mid-1960s many remote Norfolk villages were still served by delivery vans pulled by horses; today the smaller Norfolk roads twist and turn even as they did centuries ago, and every few yards along the tiniest by-road there is, it seems, a village, a hamlet, or one or two isolated houses. And in Norfolk almost every dwelling-place seems to be at least two or three hundred years old, for this is a deeply conservative county where traditions change slowly, and land is passed on carefully from father to son.

Although he is now frail and confined to a nursing home, Will's conversation still sparkles with the memory of former times: of the dusty roads, of horses, and of travellers covering a few miles a day across the lonely fields. But as Will emphasises in his broad Norfolk accent, the countryside was a busy place in his youth, where every farm employed dozens of men, and where instead of the endless arable acres of the modern landscape, farmers grew crops and kept animals.

'I was born in 1904 in Scole and I left school at twelve years old, but I was on the farm milking the cows every day from the time I was about ten. Every farm had at least a few cows then. I worked at Rose Farm at Scole when I left school – that would have been about 1916.'

Will is eager to be exact as to seasons, times and places in the past, but his memory is excellent and he can pin down the main events of his early life with enviable precision; some memories are sad and some happy, but most recall the simple drudgery of a vanished existence.

'The owner of Rose Farm died in 1922 and I had to move on. You just moved, then, in those circumstances, just got up and left; there was no dole, no social security, no redundancy money. But by then I was a pretty good ploughman. I'd learned to plough two horses side by side, which is the way we did it in Norfolk, and we used a two-furrow plough. At the ploughing time we were up at six o'clock every day, which is hard on a young boy; but we knew nothing else and got used to it, I suppose. So, we fed the horses first, on chaff and corn ground up and mashed together. That was in the stable, but when we turned them out we fed them hay which was put in the iron ricks for them. At night they were turned out into a walled yard which isn't done any more and I don't know why we did it then. But they were always put in the yard rather than in the field or kept in their stalls.

'*Then it'd be time to tackle up…*'

'I would calculate that in the Scole area there were four horses and four men to every one hundred acres of land. That's a lot of men and horses. And you imagine those numbers going right across Norfolk and probably Suffolk, too – you can imagine how many people there were in the countryside. Not like now, where each farm is lucky if it has one man, and everyone else gets in a car and dashes off to the nearest town to work. The countryside is empty today, compared to what it was when I was a young man, anyway.'

Every point is emphasised with a wave of Will's great gnarled hands, the hands of a man who has spent virtually every moment of his working life on the land. He is keen to describe exactly how the horseman's day was organised because, as he says 'we shan't see them no more'.

'After feeding the horses at six o'clock we'd have our own breakfast in the house – we'd never feed before the horses – and then it'd be time to tackle up. We had different kinds of harness for different jobs. Mostly they'd be leather, of course, but for ploughing we put chains on. I suppose the extra weight helped, although the nature of ploughing depends on the nature of the land. On the right kind of land the horses can walk away with it; on heavy clay land, though, they'd be all of a tremble, and winded halfway up a field. Often they'd stop halfway, and they'd be shaking and blowing, and you'd have to let them rest then. It was hard work even for a great strong horse on these lands. Hard work for the man, too, in all weathers, perhaps with only a sack over his shoulders to keep the rain off and miles to walk behind that plough in a day. Only on light land could you plough an acre a day; on heavy you'd be put to it to do half or three-quarters, and a man walked fourteen miles with his horses to plough one acre. It was hard work, but I never thought much of it because it was what I had to do. You just had to keep walking and you didn't think much about anything as you went along.

'Mind you, if you weren't skilled at it, your arms would be aching from holding the plough and trying to keep an eye on the horses and keeping straight and level at the same

'… in all weathers, perhaps with only a sack over his shoulders.'

time. A good man would hardly touch the handles or the horses; they'd be a real team and know what they were about, with the horses turning on the headland at a word from the ploughman, and he'd be as straight as a die up the field.'

The skill of the ploughman was a great thing in Norfolk when the horse still reigned supreme, and men would travel miles to enter a match or to compete against a known champion. Ploughing matches were partly a chance to test one's skill against all comers, but they were also important social occasions.

'Ploughing matches were a great thing round here, here and all over Norfolk. They were judged by men we called "stickers", who got the name because they carried sticks to mark the furrows. In a drawing match you'd draw one furrow only and the stickers would judge you on that, not on a whole field.

'We used old Shire horses when I was young. They were fine to work with, but in the 1920s they were gradually replaced by Suffolk Punches. Now they really were powerful great animals, though good-tempered, most of them. They were also cleaner than the old Shire horse, which was all hair, and if you didn't keep his hairy legs cleaned regularly he got all sorts of problems and went lame. And in the field while he worked he could get so bogged down with mud that he almost couldn't move, and we'd have to stop in the middle of the field to hack the mud off him to keep him going. So the Suffolk Punch was bound to take over. Yes, they were a big improvement.'

Ploughing was just one part of the horses' work: there was also carting, harrowing and sowing, though these tasks were less arduous than ploughing, as was hoeing which was also done with horses. 'We used horses to hoe the corn when it had just come up; with horse-hoeing, the man led with the horse coming behind. The main crops in my youth were wheat, barley and oats, and oats were very important because we used them for feed for the cows, sheep and horses. We also grew beans and peas. Today, of course, the farmers grow what the European Community tells them to grow and nothing else, and there's little skill in it. Plenty of chemicals, plenty of machines and that's it; not much skill at all. And not much effort either, though I suppose that has to be a good thing.

'There were a lot more cattle here in the twenties and thirties, too. When I moved to Denton in 1942 there were twenty-two people working there; now there are three. Then I was at Street Farm, a name which I always thought rather funny because there was very little in the way of a street running by the farm then. It had just forty acres, and we kept sixteen cows and a hundred pigs. I was married by this time, and when my son and daughter had grown up a bit they helped me. Farmers never took holidays in those days, they just couldn't, and it was a hard life by today's standards, I suppose. I've had five weeks holiday in total in my ninety-two years.'

There is no bitterness or envy in Will's account of his early farming days; as he says himself, he grew up at a time when you accepted your lot, when Church and state and everything you knew or came across emphasised the impossibility of avoiding your fate. If your father was a landworker or a farmer, then ninety-nine times out of a hundred that's what you would be, and it was almost sinful to think of anything else. And a boy would learn the rudiments of agriculture as they had always been learned, not in any formalised way, but simply by watching and doing simple tasks until he was ready for more. It was a system honoured simply by long usage.

Will at Street Farm just after World War II

'Yes, I learned how to farm mostly by watching other people. When I was very young I remember my father gave an old farm-worker sixpence to look after me and show me what to do. But all my family had been farmers or farm-workers for centuries and I suppose I was born to it. It just seemed to come natural to me. My father managed four farms in all, and we lived at one of the four, Rose Farm where I was born. When the owner died he wanted Dad to take over Rose Farm, which reluctantly he did. My mother died in 1924, but death was an everyday occurrence then, with little medicine and few doctors and no science; I don't think the doctors knew much at all about anything much. When the man I worked for died in 1922 I went back to work for my father. Then I got a job as a cowman at Stanton, where I got a house with the job and had about twenty cows a day to milk. It all seems very small beer now, I know, but all the farms then, like the fields themselves, were small and a man made a living, not a fortune, on a farm.'

Once he was living in his own house, Will took stock of his situation and resolved to raise enough money to rent his own farm, even though it was a rare thing in those days for a farm-worker to earn more than the absolute minimum necessary for survival. And even as he dreamed of his own farm, the long working days continued; to this day, his overriding memory of winter is of ploughing and of the harshness of the weather.

Summer memories are very different: 'My strongest memory of summer is of milking the cows and the heat, the sweat in my eyes and the flies everywhere. And of course the cows in a mood and spinning about and kicking when you tried to milk them. I was the cowman at Denton for about three years, after which I seem to recall I was much in demand, for some reason. Whatever was behind it, there were plenty of farmers willing to offer me a job – they all seemed to want my services!'

Will chuckles, then says: 'I chose the farmer at a place called Dickleburgh, not so far from Scole, where the job was to manage about a hundred acres owned by a butcher. Part of my pay was the chance to work an allotment of land, free of rent. That was a real chance then, because in the thirties farming had no money in it at all, and if I'd had to pay anything to have that bit of an allotment there'd have been no point in taking it. I cleared it of weeds – it hadn't been touched in years – and I got a little money by cultivating it in my spare time. I used to work all day on the butcher's farm, and then pull up my own beets at night by hand; I'd be at it all night with often no sleep for a week. I was there from 1922 until 1942, when I was able to take Street Farm.

'I was always very much a one-man band, and a very small farmer by today's standards, and as I've said, I only ever had my son and daughter to help. My rent in my first year at Street Farm was £28 for the half year – farm rent was paid in April and October, at Lady Day and Michaelmas. I had nothing much at all when we moved to that farm, a few sticks of furniture, a bed and little else. But my wife was able, and soon got what little we had into manageable shape.'

Although it was clearly a hard life, Will at last had a place of his own, and there was just a little more time for the pleasures of life. 'When we were young and first married it wasn't all work, and although there was no television or radio and we never went anywhere, everyone else was in much the same boat – except the toffs, of course – so it didn't matter much. I remember we played dominoes and draughts as children, but none of the houses had much light then, or heating, just a big old fire and a few candles or oil lamps a bit later on, so it was cold and dark; but I don't remember being particularly uncomfortable, and you had to go to bed early anyway, to be up early to work.

'When I was a little older I used to go to Diss at weekends to whist drives and dances, so we had some fun. We did go to pubs, too, but I always remembered my father's warning that pubs were for man's use not for man's abuse. Pubs were dingy old places in those days, full of smoke and not a woman in sight; a woman wouldn't go near a pub then because if she did, it was automatically assumed that she was a prostitute. There were no exceptions to that.'

Undoubtedly the pub was an important place of relaxation for country people, and Will's recollection of the atmosphere of the pubs he knew is remarkably vivid: 'Every pub looked more or less the same when you went in: a big fire, a few scrubbed deal tables, dark low ceilings and a few old boys sitting round with their mugs of beer and smoking hard; everyone smoked short clay pipes for all they were worth. When you went in a pub you couldn't see through the smoke some days, and people nowadays think cigarettes are bad! Mind you, with a few candles or an oil lamp the only light, it wasn't surprising you could see so little. Besides, there was nothing much to see in most pubs since people went there to drink and play cards. Things were very different then – just you imagine, you went in the pub and the first thing the landlord does is give you a pipe! That's what used to happen when he knew you.

'My father hated a new pipe, so when the landlord gave him a new one he'd straightaway give it to another old boy till it had been smoked black, then my father would have it back. He liked 'em well worn in, as he used to say; improved the flavour of the smoke.'

Many of the pub regulars were agricultural dealers, there to strike a bargain over a glass and a pipe, and this was particularly true on busy market days when many of the pubs did most of their trade. On other days the pub bar might remain empty for, as Will says, 'there

'Every pub looked more or less the same when you went in...'

were very few visitors, no tourists or holidaymakers'; it was local men or nothing. On market day, however, the men would make a big thing of the pubs:

'They would go from pub to pub. I remember one old boy. Tom Reeve, who would have been fifty or sixty when I was a boy. He used to drink in the King's Head in Scole after tying his pony and cart up outside. Well, one day it ran off and we all watched him tearing down the road after it. We had a good laugh over that!' Such small misfortunes could be a source of amusement; but eager to dispel the myth of some rural idyll, Will also remembers how quick men were to argue and even to fight with bare knuckles.

'People were a lot rougher then than they are now, and in pubs there were *always* fights, and on the least provocation. A man might knock you down just because you looked at him for a second or two too long, and the worst offence was to pick up the wrong man's beer – if you did, there was a very good chance he'd knock you down for it without a word.

'We're all a lot better behaved towards each other now, whatever the papers say. In those days some men went round deliberately looking for a fight; it was their bit of excitement, I suppose, even though they sometimes came off worse for the encounter.

'I remember once when I was a mere boy I was keeping score at dominoes for a couple of old boys in the pub. Well, I made a mistake and pegged the board wrong for one of them, and in a second he jumped up as if to hit me. But I was lucky because the landlord stopped him – and I was a just a boy, remember. I don't know why we were all like that then, but it was a common thing to fight, and the fights could be nasty.

'Perhaps it was the fact that communities were very isolated. I hardly knew anyone who'd been more than a couple of dozen miles from our area, and no one had been to London or could tell me anything about it. The roads were narrow and overgrown in most places outside the villages and they were covered with rough stones, not tar as they are now. Yes, I think it was the isolation, and the idea that a man was only worth anything if he was good with his fists – we couldn't feel good about out jobs or our cars because the former were all the same, and we didn't have any cars. Never seen 'em.'

With no responsibility for the roads beyond the parish boundary, road repair was a local matter carried out haphazardly, if at all; and that meant villages could be cut off not just by snow, but also by heavy rain which might make the smaller roads impassable for days. 'Old women were paid to pick stones from the field into heaps, and these were used on the roads,' remembers Will. 'The women got two bob a ton, I think. They had to put them in heaps and then the farmer would collect all the stones in a cart and carry them to the road where a lot of very old men, perhaps from the workhouse, were employed to break the stones into small pieces and spread them on the road. Keeping the roads in a

'… give it to another old boy until it had been smoked black.'

Old women were paid to pick stones from the field

half-decent state was almost a year-round job, because by winter there were always new potholes to fill and if they weren't filled quickly they got deeper and deeper.

'I think tar started to come in in the late 1920s, but then only for the main roads. The tar was heated up in a big iron pot pulled by horses; it was tipped onto the road and then levelled and swept back and forth by men with special brooms.'

The countryside may have been a busier place during the early years of this century, with most farms having numerous employees, but movement of goods, animals and men was expensive and it was therefore kept to a minimum. Moreover the idea of travel for the pleasure of travel itself was quite unheard of: 'Even horse traffic was scarce in the twenties asnd thirties; you could drive a cart for miles and you'd rarely pass another. Most people walked everywhere – my mum and dad didn't even have a bicycle, and only people with a fair bit of money could afford a pony and a trap. They might have a horse and cart for moving things around the place, but that was about it; my dad in his whole life never even went as far as Norwich.

'I would occasionally get a lift on the dickie seat at the back of a carriage, but they only took me along so that I could hop out whenever we reached a gate that had to be opened; but that was my travel and I enjoyed it. There were different horses kept for the different forms of transport: hackneys were for riding and showing, ponies pulled traps and small carts and, of course, there were ordinary carthorses for the heavy wagons.

'For my first few jobs as a lad I was sent all over the place to do all sorts of different jobs – I went feeding bullocks for a while, and was then sent to a shepherd at lambing time. I remember the weather was terrible, so we used what we called "lamb clothes", round hurdles designed to keep the wind off the lambs in their first few vulnerable hours. The shepherd had a tiny hut out in the fields about twelve feet square, with a wooden bench at one side and a stove that he kept burning continually with wood, and a chair where I sat, while the candle threatened to go out at any moment in the draught. The shepherd lay on the hard bench. He lived there all the time the sheep were lambing and could never wash or anything; but in those days no one worried very much about that anyway since no one had a bath in their house or even an inside loo – just a hole dug in the garden and moved when it filled up. He was brought food every day by someone in his family, and when lambing was over he left the hut for another year.

'We always had big fires at home when I was a boy, one in the kitchen and one in the living-room. Mother baked once a week on a Friday and washed on a Monday; that was the way a woman was expected to do it, and if she didn't she was considered beyond the pale. I suppose in every area of life there was a way to do things and it was strictly adhered to. Any deviation was frowned on.'

The Great War did much to weaken the old ways and the often repressive unwritten rules which governed everyday life in the English countryside, but the hard facts of life in isolated rural communities were unavoidable, and nowhere more so than in the field of medicine.

'I had four brothers and three sisters who all died in infancy,' remembers Will, 'and most families had lost little children – disease was everywhere, particularly TB and smallpox, and of course if you had no money you couldn't get a doctor even if you were dying. My father ran four miles for the doctor soon after one sister was born, and the doctor brought my father back with him in the pony cart; I remember that as if it was yesterday, though it must be nearly eighty years ago. The vet was another character who'd give you a lift if you went to get him – but he'd only do it if it was wet and you agreed to catch his pony for him first!'

Though horses are a common sight today, it is difficult to imagine just how they dominated life in town and country before the coming of the motor car. According to Will they were the backbone of all work, but they were also intimately connected with the division between the social classes.

'I remember the pub stables – every pub stables – were always lined with horses, or they'd be tied up in the street at rings fixed in the brickwork of the wall. No one we knew rode a horse around the place; that was something only the toffs could afford because you needed a saddle, bridle and a proper riding horse to do it – a hackney would cost a great deal more than a pony or a carthorse. Besides, if you'd tried it people would've thought you'd gone mad, aping the gentry, and *they* wouldn't have taken too kindly to it, either. It just wasn't for the likes of us so we didn't aspire to it.'

Agricultural wages then were very low indeed: Will's first wages as a man were nine shillings a week, and a married man got ten shillings. Men like Will's father couldn't read or write although some might manage their own name; but he and Will were luckier than many because Will's mother could write, so she kept the farm books and entered the figures in a great ledger.

'Beer cost tuppence a pint just after the Great War, but it was very hard to live. And the workhouses were always full; if you didn't or couldn't work, that's where you might well end up.' So like his fellows, Will worked most days from dawn until dusk.

'On my first farm we ploughed all but a few of the one hundred acres, all but a meadow of about six acres. We'd plough from late September until January, and when the horses weren't ploughing we'd use them to cart things. Our barley we used to sell to the maltsters for beer – we had to take it to Diss or Eye in what were known as cwmb sacks. Our cart would hold thirty sacks of wheat or barley, and thirty sacks made roughly three tons which could only be pulled by three horses. We'd travel with a load like this at about three miles an hour because we'd never trot the horses, always walk them. You'd get the sack for trotting them – that was a certainty if you were found out.

'It's easy enough to drive a great heavy wagon and three horses so long as you let the horses get on with it. I used to sit on the front of the beet wagon with the reins tied loosely on the harness: driving by mouth, we called it; in other words I'd just tell the horses what to do, and I never had to use the stick or the reins. When ploughing I used to show off by doing it with no line – with no reins, that is, and again by word of mouth. The old men didn't like it and said the horses would run away one day, but they never did. To get them to turn left we'd shout "Cum 'ere", and for right "Whisht".

'We used to go about on Saturdays to the drawing matches, and I won a lot of prizes at this. These were usually given by local tradespeople and the first prize was nearly always a copper kettle; other prizes would be tools of one sort or another. On a Saturday we might walk as far as Wortham, eight miles away. At a drawing match the horses and ploughs were already there, and you'd just draw, plough, one furrow. For ploughing matches you had to plough with your own team and you had to do a certain minimum number of furrows, perhaps twelve or twenty. It was all judged on how level your ploughing was. Bad ploughing is very easy to spot, but there wasn't much of that where we were because the ploughmen who entered the matches really knew their stuff.

'In the last days of horse-ploughing men would drive round in cars to take part in the different matches – like that they could clean up on the prizes; and then suddenly it was all over for ever, and there were no more horses and no more ploughing.'

Will worked with Shire horses

A group of 'stickers' at a Norfolk ploughing match in about 1928. 'They got the name because they carried sticks to mark the furrows.'

Away from the ploughing matches the great passion of the men was a pub game called quoits, and at one time almost every pub in Norfolk resounded to the clang of the quoits irons. Now the game has vanished almost as completely as the horse-ploughing matches. 'Quoits matches were always being played in every pub yard. A quoit is a ring of iron weighing as much as eleven pounds. There was an iron peg with a feather stuck in it that was driven into the centre of what we used to call the quoit bed, a clay area designed to make the quoits slow down or stick a bit. No money was ever bet, but a gallon or two of beer might go to the winner of a game and the loser then bought the beer. You had to throw your quoits eighteen yards and each man had two quoits. Four men would play at any one tie. The last place I saw it played was at Billingford Common in the 1950s. Like horses, it just seemed to reach the end of its days and it disappeared, but the men loved it all over Norfolk. I suppose the men who played it had done so since they were young and still enjoyed it, but by the time they passed away their sons had other interests, motorbikes and cars.'

As he nears the end of his life, Will's views are still based on an intensely practical vision of the world, a belief in the need simply to get on with living; but even in the narrow isolated environment of 1920s rural Norfolk he was also aware of other, very different lives. 'The local toff round Scole was Sir Edward Mann; he owned all the land round about and all the farmers were his tenants. I can't say he was a bad landlord, although I know many others were, but we only saw him and his family when they were pheasant shooting and we'd perhaps beat for them. They lived what seemed to us a completely cut-off sort of a life, though we never questioned it. Sir Edward's grandson is at Billingford Hall now, so it goes on. They never met their tenants because it was all done through an agent.

'I think old people had the worst of it when I was a young man. I've lived into the age of social security, but back then, if they had no one to look after them they starved or froze to death. Neighbours might help, but they could easily end in the workhouse and many would rather die in a ditch than that. It wasn't easy for women, either, particularly if they had husbands who spent all their wages in the pub. And many did, while their wives struggled to bring up twelve or thirteen children in a tiny cottage without heat or light or water as they are known today.

'Everything was different then, every detail. If you could go back in time the first thing you would notice is that everyone wore drab clothes, black or brown or some other nondescript colour. All the women wore ankle-length dresses when I was a boy, and leather, button-up boots. The men always wore hob-nailed boots made of the thickest leather, and if they got soaked they'd be as hard as hell the next morning when you came to put them on; and tough though they were, they would generally last only a year. But we wore them every day and a man only ever had the one pair. A pair of boots might cost fifteen shillings, and I reckon every working man in Norfolk wore the same sort. It wasn't until the 1930s that I got something different: lace-up rubber boots, which lasted as long as leather boots but were more comfortable. We all wore waistcoats, too – the men I mean – and special ploughman's trousers of soft thick cloth.

'My strongest memories are of the terrible struggle I had to scrape enough money together to take my own farm; I only managed it at last because I had that old allotment land rent free. I used to borrow a plough and a horse to work it, but as you know, I had no time during the day because I was working for another man. So I worked all day and then all night, without a bit of sleep. When I did rent my farm I was afraid of failing at it, but I knew I had to try, and that I would work from light till dark to make a go of it. Many days I carried 120 bags a day from the thresher to the cart, and that was a hard business because a sack might weigh two or three hundredweight.'

Harrowing

'Pigs were driven along the road...'

Will's memories stretch back beyond even the steam traction engines and binders that began to infiltrate Norfolk in the twenties and thirties, and his descriptions of some aspects of farm life have an almost eighteenth-century ring to them. 'Barley and hay and corn were all cut by hand when I first started, all done with scythes as it had been from time immemorial. The way it was done meant that the men in a field couldn't all start at once. We were very systematic about it. The headman would start mowing up the field first and one by one the others would fall in behind and to the right-hand side of him. Perhaps fifteen men would mow, and if the weather was right it would all be carted loose. There would be two on top of the cart and two on the ground forking the hay up to the men on top, and it had to be laid carefully in a circle on top of the cart because if you put it on any old way you wouldn't get much on. Four of us might cart ten acres in a day in this way, and we'd take it in to the farmyard and unload it.

'Our ricks were normally ten by five yards, roughly the height of a twenty-stave ladder, and they would have thatched roofs just like a house. To thatch the roof you'd make up what we called a yelum [yealm: meaning bundle] of straw; you'd put six yelums in a yoke [wooden fork or hod] and then tie that with rope; up on the stack a man would undo the yoke and pin it to the stack with an iron clip. Bit by bit the whole thing would be pinned and covered, nice and waterproof.

'All our milk went to Diss and from there on the train to London; we took it to the station every day, and twice a day in summertime. When we were taking cattle to market we'd drive them into Diss; in those days there were gates everywhere along the roads so they couldn't wander off into people's gardens or into fields. Pigs were driven along the road just the same and we never lost any, even when we walked them to Norwich, as occasionally we did.

'I didn't really retire till I was eighty-three, and I was married for sixty-five years; and in all that time I've never

'Milk to London by train'

been further than Denton, about twelve miles away. Never been abroad or to London, and never wanted to, really. Always plenty of pubs enough in this area! Farming's a lot easier now; the fields are bigger for the machinery, and the animals have mostly gone and the farm-workers; yet my son makes a better living than I did as a young man – and good luck to him!'

Will and his son, Ivor, ride the plough horse home

NOTE   Will Constance died in March 1995.

HIGH DAYS AND HOLIDAYS

REG DOBSON

NEWTON, WARWICKSHIRE

Amid the crowded towns and cities of the English Midlands there are occasional green oases, and tucked away in one of these and just a few miles from the busy town of Rugby is Reg Dobson's Home Farm. It has changed little since it was built three hundred or more years ago and it has a curious meandering feel to it, with staircases hidden behind doorways and bedrooms tucked away in odd corners here and there, and in under the eaves.

Reg is now in his late eighties, but he still helps his son to run their farm; and like so many traditional farmers he looks back with great fondness to the days when farming was a way of life rather than a means simply to make money. Reg has an unusual memory for the mass of incident and detail from long ago, and he is a fund of marvellous stories about the characters he knew as a boy and as a young man. Though he has farmed in Warwickshire since the 1950s he started life on a farm further west in deepest Shropshire, as he explained when I met him in his massive kitchen with its beamed ceiling and roaring fire.

'I was brought up at a place called Cheswardine Park at Market Drayton; I had one brother and four sisters, and I was the eldest. We had a big old house, and it always seemed to be crowded with people; I think all farmhouses were well filled in those days because so many people worked on the land, and by tradition they lived in with the farmer and his family. So as well as us children and my parents we had a nursemaid, a kitchenmaid, my aunt Katy and her son George.

'My mother was a very kindly woman, and although she died when I was only nine I remember her well. One thing that was particularly unusual about her was that she would not tolerate any cruelty to the farm animals – that may not sound so special now, but in those days people cared a lot less about animal welfare.

'On Saturday nights we were always bathed in a tin bath in front of a massive log fire. I remember I once refused to get undressed, so the nursemaid undressed me; but when she turned her back I bolted through the back door and out into the pitch-dark garden – after a long chase I was caught, however, and carried back to the house.

Reg takes great delight in talking about the past, and he has a genuine ability to bring it alive: 'I can't remember ever really falling out with my brothers and sisters, though I do remember once making my sister eat coal, which we used to feed to the pigs for the minerals! We used to walk across the fields to school unless it was very wet, and then mother or one of the girls in the house took us in the pony and trap. We loved that.

'Horses were a big part of my life because Dad had made a lot of money during the Great War by selling horses. We were quite well dressed and shod, unlike a lot of children and adults at that time. Mother used to give the poor our old clothes and shoes. We had hens, and in those days of course every hen in the country was free range – they just wandered about the yard and we fed them on wheat and maize. However, the grain used to attract hundreds of sparrows and this annoyed us, so we used to catch them by tying a long piece of string to a coal riddle and propping it up on a stick. We'd then put a pile of corn under the riddle and when a sparrow landed we'd pull the string, down would come the riddle and we'd catch it! We used to give them to Mother who made them into pies.

'We were terrible then for using catapults – all country boys were – and we'd fire at anything and everything, I'm afraid. Mostly, though, we'd fire at empty glass bottles; in those days they used to have a marble inside, so when we'd broken the bottle with the catapult we'd collect the marbles. We became experts at marbles, my brother and I.

'After my mother died Father was away virtually all the time dealing in horses, land or one thing and another.

'One of my best childhood memories was of visits to my maternal grandparents. Grandma always made a big fuss of me, and for some reason she always insisted on buying my boots for me, I think perhaps because she'd worn shoes that were too tight when she was a girl. As a result she had to have a toe amputated when she was eighty – and without anaesthetic! I remember she just lay there and I held her hand while they cut off her toe: she never made a sound.

'We were terrible then for using catapults…'

'Just before she died she lay in bed and pointed to a drawer in an old cupboard and said to me, "When I die, all the money in that drawer is for you." Alas, I never got a penny of it, because as soon as she died the housekeeper rifled the drawer and disappeared for ever with all the money!'

Reg's family have been farmers on both his mother's and his father's side for generations. His maternal grandfather was also a trained blacksmith and shod all his own horses on the farm. He had a great fondness for beer, too; every Wednesday he'd set off for Market Drayton, as Reg recalls:

'He'd always take the horse and waggon – or float as we used to call it – and he'd invariably take his neighbour, who was an old friend, with him. They'd put the horse up at the pub – every pub had stables then – and proceed to get gloriously drunk. At chucking out time the publican would help them out of the door and into the waggon, then he'd lead the horse into the middle of the street and away they would go. They would soon fall fast asleep and the horse would slowly make his way home five miles away; he would walk into the yard where he would stop, then my grandma would come out to wake the two men up and give them a good telling-off. The telling-off never did any good, though, because the following week they'd be off again.'

Market Drayton seemed to be alive with characters like Uncle Arthur: 'He was one of the first in our area to get a car, though it was such an old banger that a horse had to pull it before it would start. He once drove all the way to Bishop's Castle on the wrong side of the road; if he met a waggon or another car (very rare) he would simply curse and yell at the other driver as if it was *his* fault that we were on the wrong side of the road!'

But apart from odd moments of hilarity, life in Shropshire in the early part of this century tended to be hard and unremitting, and this produced a tough independence of character, typified by Reg's father. 'Dad was a very fierce man; he had only to look at us and say "That will do", and we were terrified into silence. He'd taken over Cheswardine Park from his mother when she died, leaving him ten young brothers and sisters to look after. At the time, Cheswardine was in a very poor state, as were most farms in the twenties; but when he sold it years later it was one of the best farms in Shropshire. He was a tough, determined man.'

Inevitably horses were an important part of young Reg's life, and to this day he retains a keen interest in horse racing; for his father, however, horses were everything. 'He was horse mad: he just loved them, whether riding, driving or buying and selling them. I remember he bought two really good ponies for me – they were a bit wild, but that's what people wanted in those days; they only wanted quiet ones for the trap or cart, but lively ones to carry them around the place.

'I remember one filly we had which was kept in a loosebox between two cowsheds; every night and morning we gave her about a gallon of milk straight from the cow. At about eighteen months Father took her to a racing trainer becase she was such a likely looking horse; three months later she was dead from TB. She was rotten with it through and through. TB was rife in those days; we always lost two or three cows each year from TB, but people just accepted that it was a part of life then. It was called John's disease. Why *we* didn't get it I'll never know, particularly as my father would never get rid of a sick cow – he'd always assume it would get better if you left it long enough.

'Dad was into livestock of all kinds. He used to breed greyhounds now and then, for example, and one of them won several races so my father sold it for a good price; it never won again! Animals were right at the heart of our lives, and we associated them with work as well as with good fun. For instance when we were very young we used to love to ride in the heavy carts when the men were bringing in the roots or mangels – though farms could

be just as dangerous then as they are now; my sister fell out of a cart once and the great heavy wheel ran over her hand and completely crushed it. And then Father had a hell of a game getting the teachers at the school to let Dorothy learn to write with her left hand – in those days you had to write with your *right* hand even if it didn't work!' Soon it was time for Reg to go to boarding school, which he hated. 'I went from the village school to Adams Grammar School in Newport. The masters were very strict, and I was caned regularly; one master, Tubby Gill, used to beat us till we couldn't sit down! I left after four years, which was the best thing that ever happened to me. I was sixteen and started work full-time on the farm, which I loved.'

Escape from school might seem every schoolboy's dream come true, but for Reg it meant long hours and hard work – he was expected to work seven days a week, from six in the morning till six at night. There were 125 cows to milk by hand every day: 'Unless you've actually done that yourself you can have no idea of the work involved' he says now. 'There were twelve of us did the milking, and we did it according to a number system so that each person had his or her fair share of difficult cows – you know, cows that held their milk up or that kicked like hell. If they thought they could get away with it, people would deliberately take a long time at an easy cow until they could see that another easy one was next in line to be milked. We used to put a special leather strap on the kickers to keep their legs still, though some started to kick before you even got near them.

'An old man called Punch used to carry off the pails of milk as they were filled. He wore a great wooden yoke, like you'd put on a pair of oxen, with a pail hung on each side.

'In my first year I had to do the sheep, too, mostly Cheviots, and the devil to catch because we had no proper pens. I used to get the dog to hold them in a corner of the field

'In the first year I had to do the sheep, too…'

(Above) Learning from the mole-catcher: a land-girl at work in the Usk Valley early in the 1940s

(Right) Country blacksmith Bill Danson shoeing Duke, a massive Shire horse, and one of the few working horses remaining in the early 1960s

and then run in and catch the one I wanted. Half the time it was a question of run in and dive at a fleeing sheep, a bit like a rugby tackle. An old local poacher called Jim Carne used to come at shearing time. I used to turn the handle of the wheel that drove the shears – we'd come on a bit from simple hand-shears – and he did the clipping. He was very good at it, but it was hard work for a sixteen-year-old turning that thing all day.

'If you had any hope of surviving on a Shropshire farm early this century you had to be a shrewd dealer. Selling your produce in the days before intervention buying by the EC was the severest test of a farmer's ability in the market place. Dad was a sharp one for selling sheep. He'd buy them and get us to trim them and clean them till they looked really smart and then he'd take them straight back to market and usually get a pound or two more for each one than he'd paid for them.'

Self-sufficiency was important at a time when many farms were part of isolated communities, and much of the 300 gallons of milk a day the Dobsons' cows produced went to make cheese. The cheese was made on site by a cheesemaker who lived in with the family; nothing was ever wasted, and the large quantities of whey, a by-product of the cheesemaking process, were stored and then fed to the pigs: 'It was kept in a big brick tank and I used to take it by bucketful to feed the pigs. I had a yoke on my shoulders which made it a bit easier, but it was incredibly hard work, particularly on your legs. In those days we had what would now be considered very unbalanced rations for the animals – we'd prepare a great barrow full of maize-germ meal and tip it in the pigs' trough, and then we'd pour the whey on top; there was an awful lot got trodden in and slopped about. These days animal feeding is a very scientific business.

'Father always used to buy the biggest pigs…'

'Most of the feed we were able to buy came on the train to Drayton which was three miles away, and it was a full day's work to take a cart there to collect the feed and get it back to the farm.

'Father always used to buy the biggest pigs he could find; they'd weigh seven or eight stone when he brought them home, and then we'd feed them till they weighed seventeen or eighteen stone apiece. When we took them to market they were really big, in fact one was so fat that it dropped dead as it walked up the ramp into the cart! I went with Father once to Welshpool and he bought every single pig in the market. One lot in a pen had great long snouts and I didn't think they'd do any good. "They're the best of the bunch," he said, and he was right.'

The pig was the great saving of many farmers and smallholders. It was a hardy animal that grew quickly and could be relied on to hoover up any and every kind of vegetable waste with enthusiasm and turn it into delicious bacon.

'We loved it when we killed a pig,' remembers Reg, 'which may sound terrible, but you have to remember that a lot of people went hungry in those days and there was no time for sentimentality. When we killed a pig we ate every last bit of it. We had the liver and kidneys, and sausages and pork pies were made from some bits, pork scratchings from the skin. We even used the bladder, as with a bit of effort you could turn it into a really good football. You just blew it up and tied a knot in it and it lasted for ages!'

Reg Dobson has a positive, no-nonsense outlook, and is dismissive of what he sees as fads and fancies among townsfolk. 'Today, all the talk is about animal fat killing you. Well, let me tell you, we lived on it. For breakfast we'd have two eggs, six rashers of fat bacon and fried bread with masses of dripping, and this would be after porridge with huge dollops of cream all over it. Mind you, we had to work like blazes so I suppose we worked it off; and we've all lived to a pretty ripe old age, too, except my brother Lionel who was only forty-three when he died.'

Standards of hygiene on those Shropshire farms would shock many people today, but with water available only from a well, and no mains gas or electricity, a big family had to take a far more practical view of these matters. 'After a day's work in the farmyard we'd be covered in muck of one sort or another, but we only rarely had a change of trousers. Trousers were just trousers and we wore them all the time whatever their state – and there were no wellies or overalls. When you came in you just sat by the fire and the muck dried on you and steamed away. No one thought anything of it, it was just the way things were.'

There is no doubt, too, that you had to be very ill indeed to be excused a day's work, even if you were the farmer's son. 'I had serious problems with my left hip when I was a young man; it was displaced, and eventually the doctor told my father I should not carry anything heavy – but I still had to work, and had to help old Jack with the cows. Jack was an old soldier who had a bad right leg, and I often thought we must have looked a lovely couple walking across the farmyard, him limping one way and me the other!'

A typical day for Reg would start at 5.30am: he would put hay in the racks at the head of each cow's stall, and then the milking would begin, and 'No one under the age of sixty or seventy will remember what it was like to feed and muck out 125 cows every day,' he says with a wry smile. Women and men would start work together in the mornings; after breakfast they would let the cattle out to water, as none was piped to the farm in those days, and then roots and mangolds would be mixed together with corn and mash as feed. 'There was no cattle cake in those days, I'm afraid,' says Reg. 'Then we'd muck out. That was a perilous job, I can tell you, because we always seemed to have so little straw and the muck was almost liquid. We used to load it into a barrow and then push the barrow on to the top of the midden, where we tipped it. After a few years the midden might be twelve feet high, and at that height with a slippery muck-covered plank there were bound to be accidents. I've slipped off that plank many times and ended up waist-deep in cow muck!

'After cleaning out, we fed the cows individually, and you had to be smart while you were at it or the greedy ones ate up first and then started knocking the others around. There was also the risk of being kicked; if you were, in those days you'd belt the cow with a stick or with the milking stool, though eventually I realised that this made them worse, and that if you were kind and gentle they responded in the same way. Nowadays we never put a stick on our animals.'

Reg's memories of Cheswardine Park are characterised by his sense of camaraderie and good fun, the spirit of enjoyment that seems to have survived in spite of the long hours of hard work in all weathers. Many of the men and women Reg worked with became friends for life, and one or two, like Reg Boffey, married into the family.

'Reg eventually married one of my sisters; he used to cut the hay while I forked it in to the animals, and we had great fun together, but he was a devil for cutting the wads bigger and bigger. They'd start at about a yard square and soon be two yards square, and the more he could get on the pikel the better he liked it. One day I just managed to stagger out of the barn with a massive load he'd put on my fork, then collapsed in the yard with all the hay on top of me. I didn't think much of it, but he fell about laughing.

'We were always playing good-natured jokes on each other and on the others. I remember Frank Chidlow who used to cart for us – we used to fill his cart so full of muck at muck-spreading time that his horse couldn't budge it an inch. We thought it was hilarious, even though we straightaway had to lessen the load to get the thing moving; either that or Frank would go and get what we called a chainhorse to help pull the cart. And he'd cuss his head off at us while he did it.

'When he was courting a girl at Northwich Reg used to get back to the farm in the early hours, and he'd shake me and say "Sam, it's time to get up!" I'd leap out of bed in a panic, and he'd immediately jump into the warm place I'd made in the bed. We were both called Reg, but for some reason we called each other "Sam" all the time, Lord knows why. We used to share the same bed, and the room had two windows which we kept open winter and summer however hard the weather. Some mornings the jerry would be frozen over it got so cold.'

Like many rural areas, Shropshire had its fair share of eccentrics, frequently elderly, often highly superstitious men and women who had spent their lives in tiny out-of-the-way cottages, eking out a living by occasional or seasonal farm-work. 'Pay was very low in the twenties and thirties. A man would get just a few shillings a week, his wife less, even if she came to milk night and morning. Apart from Sunday, the farm-workers had only one day a year off – Good Friday, but even then they had to come and milk. However, they'd get a cottage with a big garden so they grew all the vegetables they needed, and they

Reg Dobson (seated centre) poses with fellow farmworkers in the yard at Cheswardine Park, about 1929

usually kept a pig – and that was all the meat a poor man ever got, except for rabbits.

'Frank Chidlow, our waggoner, had eight children and little money, so when he wanted a beer he'd catch himself a dozen or more rabbits and exchange them for a few pints at the local pub. When he'd had a few pints he'd start to sing, which the other regulars loved, so they'd start buying him drinks to keep him going. He'd get back to the farm at three in the afternoon, have his dinner and then go to milk; half-an-hour later he'd be fast asleep on the milking stool. Frank's wife, Olive, used to milk, too; when she was pregnant she'd milk until the day before she went into labour, and she'd be back at work the day after the child was born.'

The pub was very much the centre of social life in Reg's youth, and men would walk out miles every evening to drink at their favourite local – which might be five or six miles away if they lived in one of the many remote cottages. The pub gave men their only chance to escape the drudgery of everyday life; for the price of a few pints they could enjoy a temporary escape into a world of laughter and good fellowship.

Another pastime Reg recalls was the tug-o-war: 'We used to have horseback tug-o-wars with teams from the various farms and big houses competing. We had one once at the big house where Colonel Donaldson Hudson lived, the local squire; he entered a team, as did the surrounding farms, and we got to the final where we had to pull against the Colonel's team.

'As we got going and took up the strain, one of our horses started misbehaving; so Father put his coat over her head to calm her, but that made her worse and she reared. Bubber, a wild old boy and a great giant of a man, slipped off her – everyone was riding bareback – but we still held our own. Then seizing his chance, Bubber leapt back on, gave an almighty heave and all the Colonel's men and horses were pulled over. So we'd won; but we were disqualified because you had to let the Colonel's team win. That was the way they thought in those days.

'We used to get our own back on him, though, by laying trails of raisins the day before he was to have a big shoot; the raisins, which pheasants love, led to our wood and of course as a result we had plenty of pheasants!

'Eating competitions were a big thing in my youth in Shropshire, and I believe this was true of many other country districts; I suppose it was good, simple entertainment when we had little else. The waggoner on a farm near us was a phenomenal eater, and people used to come and fetch him to eat for bets. One night a farmer knocked at his door and asked

his wife if he would come and eat a whole calf for a bet. She wasn't in the least surprised by the request, but didn't know if he would because he'd already gone out to eat two ducks down at the Fox for a bet. "I'll go down there and ask him," said the man. He found Bill, put the proposition to him and Bill, having eaten his ducks, went off straightaway and ate the calf as well!'

Food was thus a source of great entertainment as well as being one of life's great pleasures, although one or two food sources – most notably rabbit – were not highly thought of at all; perhaps because there were so many of them and they were considered the staple of the very poorest, few liked the idea of dining regularly on rabbits. But if you found yourself in a tight corner financially you could always catch enough rabbits to earn a few bob: 'It was no trouble in those days to catch a hundred rabbits in a day – they were everywhere, and I think most of the men on the farm virtually lived on rabbit. A great friend of mine called Cyril used to be mad about cricket, just as I was, and once we went and caught rabbits and sold them until we had enough money to get to Old Trafford on the train to watch England play the Australians.'

Killing rabbits and pigs, and twisting the necks of chickens for the pot, were all part of the less-than-idyllic farming scene which held sway earlier this century; and 'closeness to nature' probably contributed to what Reg still describes as a 'a kind of roughness of character. There's no doubt we were a rough bunch in some ways: I remember one girl used to tease Cyril and me, so we picked her up and dropped her in a barrel of treacle – well, you've never seen such a sight in your life, she could hardly walk; but she never teased us again.

'We were positively medieval in our attitudes to hygiene in those days, too. I don't think it was so much that we didn't care, it was just that without running water, plastic overalls and all the other modern hygiene aids, you just had to accept that things were going to be done as they'd always been done. For example, I've explained how the cows were let out into the fields to water before we had water piped to the sheds. Well, as they went out through the narrow gateways where all the muck and slurry would accumulate, inevitably they got into a terrible mess. But we used to wipe their udders with just an old piece of sacking, and you can imagine what the milk was like after that! When we stopped making cheese on the farm we started to sell the milk to the chocolate company Nestlé, and the colour of the milk was like chocolate when we sent it to them! They were always writing to Father to complain, so we started washing the cows properly; but I don't think it really made a lot of difference.

'We were only in this position because we didn't have all the modern conveniences. Take haymaking, for example: younger people on farms today have no idea what a hard job haymaking used to be. Frank Chidlow would go out with the horses at 3am because he needed to work virtually twenty-four hours a day to get the job done in time; and of course in summer it was cooler working at that time in the morning. Actually Frank loved the horses and he'd often arrive earlier than he needed just to groom them all properly.

'When I moved here in the fifties, Frank came and sowed a field of oats for me. It ran by Watling Street, and he put a stick at either end to get a straight line and made a hell of a fuss before starting because, as he said, "I'm not having anybody go up the Watling and say, what a mess that field is!" ' At a time when ordinary men and women had few

Raking up the stooks: 'When it was ready we pitched it into the waggon by hand.'

possessions of any note, their greatest pride lay in their work and in what other people thought of their efforts. As Reg observed: 'Oh, yes, when I was young all the men would walk all round the different farms on a Sunday, and if any field had been badly ploughed or sown it would be all over the village in no time. Today no one minds what a field looks like, so long as it is all done quickly.'

It is difficult nowadays to conceive the level of poverty at which most agricultural workers once lived. Reg describes how Frank Chidlow and his wife and eight children all survived on £2 a week in a tiny cottage. 'How he did it I'll never know, but they all grew up strong and well,' he says.

If the men were indomitable, with rich, idiosyncratic characters, the same was certainly true of many of the farm animals: 'They were real characters. I remember one of our cows had a massive udder, or bag as we used to call it; we used to have to get two people to milk her, one on each side. She was a gentle thing, though; once when we had four orphaned lambs we put two on each side of this massive udder and she stood quite still and let them feed. She reared them, too, and they used to follow her about everywhere when we turned them out into the spinney.'

The labour-intensive nature of milking and of dealing with pigs and other farm animals was matched by the almost complete absence of technology on the arable fields. 'For our one hundred acres of hay, all we had in the way of implements was a turner, a device drawn by a horse that flipped the hay over so that it would dry evenly, and an old horse-rake. After the hay had been dragged up into piles we'd cock it up by hand into small heaps to keep the rain off as much as possible. Next day, or soon after, it had all to be shaken out and turned again by hand. When it was ready to cart, we pitched it onto the waggon by hand, one man on top, one each side of the waggon. Then we had to rope it on because the old cart-tracks were a bit rough and the bumps as we went along might otherwise have thrown the whole lot off. Back in the yard we pitched it into the hayloft by hand, and we'd often be at it until midnight or beyond.

'All the men were real artists when it came to hay, and hated slap-happy methods. Haymaking used to last from about mid-June to about the end of August.'

Rain was an obvious problem at haymaking time, but too much sun could also make it difficult, as Reg recalls: 'I remember Frank Chidlow cut me a fourteen-acre field of hay one year, and it was so hot that before I could get it in cocks it was already over-made – that is, too dry. We started to cart it in the horse waggon, but we had a heck of a game because it was so brittle – it started to fall off every time we had half a load on, and I don't think there was much goodness left in it anyway.

'Another time we were in the local pub one Sunday and we decided that after our dinner we would carry Harry Robinson's field – all the men helped each other at harvest time. Anyway, the pub was full, and after we'd had our fill we all trooped out and set to, eleven of us with the horses and waggons. I helped build the rick with the others pelting the sheaves up to us at a terrific rate. We did it very fast, but what a mess we had at the end of it! The rick was leaning towards the road at an angle of about 45 degrees and we had to get every pole from a radius of about a mile to prop it up! It was such a sight that someone sketched it and hung the picture in the pub that night!'

Cheswardine Park was a long way from the nearest town and with four girls and three young men living in close proximity, relationships were bound to develop, and pregnancy and scandal were never far away. 'If a girl got pregnant in those days it was a terrible disgrace. I had to pay five shillings a week for eighteen years to one young girl I made pregnant. She had the child and I paid the money, but I've never seen either of them since. I was only a lad at the time. I remember, too, that three of our bailiffs married three of our cheesemakers and Dad helped set them up on farms of their own. He was always doing that sort of thing. He lent them £250 apiece, but only one ever paid him back: he sent Father £500 about twenty years after marrying and taking his loan – Dad was highly delighted.

'Another great character was Tom Bennett, the champion hedge-layer of the whole of Shropshire. If he didn't get first prize for the best hedge-laying one year he'd get it for the best grown hedge the next. Every job he did was perfect. He used to cut our lawn with a scythe as good as any modern lawn-mower could do it. He was a great rick-builder, too, and when he'd finished he'd often come back at night to pull out the loose bits of hay just to make sure it looked perfect.

'Tom used to chew tobacco twist and he was a deadly accurate spitter – he once hit a cat on the head at about twenty feet! And he had amazing teeth; he used to bite into an iron railing at the bottom of the garden and swing from it. Tom never went anywhere in his whole life, to the best of my knowledge, except one trip after he retired when he got the bus to the Royal Show at Lincoln; but he got lost, missed the bus back, and spent £20 – a small fortune – on a taxi to get home. That was the first and last time he went anywhere!'

One theme that runs throughout Reg's endless series of delightful anecdotes is that in country districts in days gone by, people almost invariably made their own entertainment, and often this meant playing jokes on each other, which was all usually taken in good part. 'I remember two fat butchers used to call at Charlie Denton's place in a pony and trap. They were so fat that when they got in the trap the horse was nearly lifted up in the air. One day Charlie's boys undid the horse's belly strap and as soon as the butchers got in the trap the shafts shot up in the air and they tumbled out into the road. We roared with laughter, but the air was blue with the butchers' curses.

'But country people could be very stick-in-the-mud, too. I remember we had a parish meeting when the council said they would pipe water to the village houses. The older inhabitants didn't want it because they said you could smell the ducks from Stamford Park when you turned the taps on (Stamford Park was the municipal lake where the water would come from). But in spite of all, the water came in the end, and so did electricity.

'After my mother died aunt Katy looked after us. She was lovely, and I think she loved my father but he loved somebody else – the local publican's daughter. She got divorced so she could marry Dad, which cost Dad £3,000, an absolute fortune in those days. After they were married they took a hotel in Liverpool for a while, but Dad hated it. In those days you had to be whiter than white to get a publican's licence, and because my stepmother was a divorcee she couldn't get the licence; it had to be in someone else's name. But by 1931 Dad was back on a farm; he just wasn't suited to city life.'

'A chap called Walter Thomas used to work for us and he was a wonderful workman. He liked piecework, and he and his wife used to dig our potatoes. They'd dig eleven square roods a day, which is some going, and while they were doing it they used to camp in the field. Walter also used to pull our swedes, and he was so fast there'd be one landing on the heap, one flying through the air and one in his hand. He'd go on like that all day, and when we were all hoeing together he'd leave us standing if he felt like it.

'Millions of poppies'

'In winter he cut our hedges. He used a short-handled slasher, and as he was six feet tall and our hedges were rather small he could cut both sides as he went along simply by leaning over. As he cut, so his wife gathered the brashings and piled them up and burned them. They were a great team, but all they got for the work was 3d a rood. By working all the hours God sends – milking, hoeing, drilling, sowing and ploughing – they only made about £16 a week.'

It is important to remember that although Reg was officially the boss's son, there was no significant difference between his daily routine and that of the other farm-workers; they simply mucked in together. The only material difference was the fact that the farmer's son didn't get paid at all since his return would come in the long-term when he inherited the farm. This seems to have been pretty universal practice among all except gentlemen farmers with considerable sums of money.

Because he wasn't paid by his father, Reg had to find other ways to make money. 'I used to go long-netting for rabbits with Walter. One night we got fifty in one go. We also set traps, which I admit was very cruel and I'm glad it's stopped now. Country people did like eating rabbit, although if they had nothing else they got a bit tired of it. We used to go to a local dance sometimes after rabbiting, but we smelled so strong of rabbits that none of the girls would dance with us. Never mind, we used to say, we can still get into the bar!'

Reg's tales of what was obviously a lively and generally happy farming community are not based on a rose-tinted view of the past. As well as the fun and the practical jokes, things could be difficult in a way that many of us find difficult to imagine today. 'In farming it certainly wasn't all good in the old days, and at times it was very difficult indeed to make ends meet. Before the Milk Marketing Board was set up, we had to take our milk to a cheesemaker nearby and got 4½d per gallon for it; after the MMB that went up to 8½d. Selling privately and locally, as we had to do then, had some advantages but it would mean penury for the small farmer today.

'Farming was difficult and even dangerous in other ways, too – we often used to hear about people being fatally injured by their animals. It nearly happened to me once when we were leading a dangerous bull into a stall. Just as I reached down to put his chain on he whipped round and knocked me to the ground. He then knocked Jim, my stockman, over and started butting the stall. I was lucky and managed to crawl away, but either or both of us could easily have been killed.

Sheep farming has always played an important part in the rural economy on the higher moor; (below) a shepherd feeds an orphan lamb, and (right) tending the flock during a spell of bitter winter weather

On the edge of Dartmoor, just a few miles from the quiet market town of Chagford and hidden away in an all-too-easy-to-miss fold in the hills, lies Batworthy Farm. A long, gaunt-looking stone farmhouse, it is older than anyone seems able to guess; it was there when the Domesday Book was compiled, although then it was almost certainly an ancient house. The lane that approaches the farm is probably as narrow and twisting, and assuredly just as deep as it was centuries ago, for Batworthy Farm has been all but left behind by the modern world and its present owner, seventy-three year old Joe White, wouldn't have it any other way. He came to the farm with his parents seventy years ago and has been there ever since, sharing it now with his seventy-six year old sister Annie. The boundaries of his world are Chagford and Moretonhampstead, both just a few miles away, and of course the neighbouring farms, and in his long life Joe has strayed outside Devon only once; he has never been abroad, never learned to drive, and has never taken a holiday away from the farm.

His parents came to Batworthy from another long-hidden farm at Wiveliscombe in Somerset. Joe has no children of his own and is therefore the last of generations of farmers; and he farms with deliberate and conscious purpose just as his ancestors farmed – his one concession to the twentieth century is an old tractor bought more than twenty years ago by his father. He has never used chemicals or nitrates on his land, maintaining that these 'make the grass grow too fast to be any good', and only gave up using horses in the mid-1960s. He was one of the last farms to give them up and it pained him greatly to do it: 'You can't beat a horse. A horse is a wonderful animal and don't let anyone tell you t'otherwise – even ploughing with a horse wasn't as hard as people make out. It's just quicker with a tractor, but why that's such a great thing I don't understand. It's all fast and faster today, but what this rushing is all for, I don't know. Everyone wants to do everything in a hurry. Why? What are they going to do with all the time they'll have left?'

The pace of Joe's life is assuredly in tune with the pace of the seasons and the land he farms – a cliché often applied to rural lives, but never more justly used than in this instance. And horses matched that pace as the tractor and other modern contrivances never can; Joe's father always kept a good pony to ride into Chagford, and there were always at least three horses for ploughing and general use. And in the ancient stone barns dotted about Joe's 100-acre farm are still the carts and ploughs, winnowing machines and mechanical potato pullers that his father and grandfather used. If you ask him why he keeps them, he will look at you as if you are mad because, as he says, 'no real farmer would get rid of 'em – I might use 'em again. Most of them still work and you never know, I might *have* to use them again!'

Joe's main barn is as big as the house itself, and is situated just across the deep narrow lane that passes the farm; it has certain features which indicate that it was used as a house long before the present house was built: gigantic beams hold up the talet floor, boards two feet wide curving across above the beams. They curve, each one fitting the other at exactly the same angle, because they were cut one after another from the trunk of the same vast tree. Also, giant granite chimneys rear up at either end of the barn, their lintels made from massive, squared-off sections of oak. Neither house nor barn has mains electricity. 'We're not on the electricity here because they wanted twenty thousand pounds to put up ten poles to get it here!' says Joe, with a grin.

Another barn, made from equally huge blocks of roughly dressed stone, contains an ancient cider-making press and apple crusher. The great wooden wheel on the press with its enormous wooden teeth was all made by hand, each piece slotted into its rightful place with consummate skill by long-dead craftsmen. Even Joe has no idea how old the press is, but it was in use until just a few years ago and Joe only gave it up because there were so few farmers and friends left with whom he could share the cider. 'All the farms, or most of 'em anyway, come up for sale when the old folks die, and they're bought by Londoners who come down and try to tell us how to do things. The children go away to college and don't come back, so the farms have all gradually been sold to strangers. It's a pity, but the world's all wrong and I suppose there's nothing we can do about it.'

In between regular and copious bouts of snuff-taking – he has enjoyed J. & H. Wilson's Special No 1 for more than half a century – Joe showed me round his ancient farm. First the big granite barns, then up the hill towards another half-hidden, overgrown barn where an old Syracuse horse plough lay, carefully tended and left in good order, just as it was left when Joe last ploughed with horses: 'You could take 'im out tomorrow, just as good as he always was. The local priest had to come to *me* for the plough-blessing ceremony – wouldn't do with a *modern* plough, would it?' He laughs, and we move on to look at an old, hand-operated winnowing machine, which Joe describes in great and loving detail. 'All this was brought in in my father's time, and it worked very well so I kept it. Those big machines that do the whole lot, you know, you have to destroy the farm to get them in! And what do I want all that for? All that noise and black smoke everywhere. That's not farming, that's a sort of factory work, and it's not for me.'

The most noticeable thing about Batworthy Farm – apart from its beauty, and the intimate nature of its fields and hedges – is the clean smell: the smell of summer, and hay in the making; the smell of the small-scale enterprise; the gentle. Even the few cattle, the basis of all Joe's efforts for many years, have a quieter, less intensive aura than modern breeds.

'They're South Devons, rare animals now, but in fact just what you're supposed to have in South Devon', says Joe with a wink. 'Of course, Londoners come down and tell us to get Limosines or whatever they're called, 'cos they work out with a pencil and paper or a calculator that they can make more money with 'em, or some damn thing. No, I've always kept South Devons and I'm not changing now. They're lovely animals and as good as any other – better than most, and Father kept the same cows so the strain goes right back. Of course, other people always have to go for the fancy and foreign, but they don't really know what they're on about. They come down and tell us what to do, but *I* tell *them* if I get the chance!'

Further up the field Joe stands proudly looking over a day-old calf lying near its mother in the warm sun. We cross that field and enter another, and Joe has names for them all: Barn Hill, Cows Flat, Barn Park – and there are many fields in spite of the fact that the farm amounts to little more than 120 acres; but then, few fields extend to more than a few acres. 'This field has eleven gates,' he says, 'and what a useful thing that is! We can move the cows around easily and simply between one field and the next, nip in here and out

Joe's brother at the ancient cider press

'They're South Devons, rare animals now…'

there; no fuss and never far to go to get to the next gate. What's the point of huge great fields you can hardly see across – nothing but more trouble and bother, and I suppose there's money behind it.'

Another granite building once housed a stone walkway to allow a horse to go round in endless circles pulling a chaff cutter mechanism; in it, Joe showed me the cart his father once used every week to take the farm produce to market in Chagford: 'It's just as my father left it. We call it a butt cart or a tip-up cart, because' he says with a smile 'when there's no horse in the shafts it tips right over! We used to take it regularly into town till quite recently. Look what a beautiful made thing it is. Each joint in the wheels and frame hand-made.' And he's right, it is a marvellous thing, its curved sides, runner and bottom boards fitting together perfectly. Through the blister of many years' sun and rain the still sturdy cart carries the name and address, carefully inscribed, of Joe's father.

Up in another of Joe's little fields on the edge of the hillside a second small group of sad-eyed cattle flick their tails in the heat, allowing Joe to come within inches of their noses, even though they are rather nervous, having only recently calved. The scene has all the calm dignity of farming as carried on as a living craft, rather than a business, and the cattle seem to reciprocate this feeling of respect as they allow Joe to pat a calf just a few days old. Joe's attitude to his animals is matched by his attitude to the appearance of the farm:

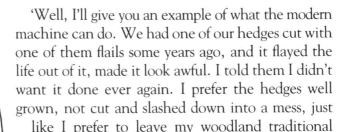

'Well, I'll give you an example of what the modern machine can do. We had one of our hedges cut with one of them flails some years ago, and it flayed the life out of it, made it look awful. I told them I didn't want it done ever again. I prefer the hedges well grown, not cut and slashed down into a mess, just like I prefer to leave my woodland traditional because this gives a bit of cover for the wildlife and the foxes – I used to be a great hunting man! We boys used to get out together after the old fox, and what good times we had! You need a bit of woodland for foxes. I used to love the gymkhanas, too, and used to ride the old pony over to them wherever they were, for a laugh and a bit of talk. Even going into Chagford each week was a bit of fun, because we'd meet all the other good old boys and have a yarn and an argument. But there are few of us left now, except at the Chagford Show.

'So much has changed – you take families. When I was young all the families were big, there might easily be fifteen children in a family and they'd all help one another.'

The old ways die slowly in this part of Devon. Fuel for the range in the house and for the fires has never had to be bought in, for example, because with plenty of well-grown hedgerows and bits of woodland dotted about the place, Joe and Annie are well able to stock up for the winter.

'There's always windfalls and we cuts a bit of timber here and there,' explains Joe, 'though you'd never notice we'd taken it. Plenty of wood hereabouts.'

Joe laughs a lot and his glorious Devon accent takes some getting used to, but he is a kindly man, small and neat of stature, whose nature seems to match the quiet of his working life. Annie, his sister, sits on an upturned basin in the lane that runs by the farm. She returned to the farm where she had spent her childhood after her husband died; now she helps with the cattle and with Joe's other great passion, his vegetable patch, where neat rows of onions and potatoes grow quickly in the sheltered valley. 'I grow a lot of my vegetables for competitions at the Chagford Show,' he explains. 'They give prizes for the biggest onions, and the biggest leeks and carrots, though I bother mostly for the talk and the argument.' They are virtually self-sufficient in vegetables, and the few chickens which wander happily about the yard provide eggs and meat. 'So we don't need much to live on, and we certainly don't need money for holidays 'cos we don't have any! I like my holidays here – after the harvest there's always a bit of time. I've never gone away from here because anywhere else it's all going too fast, and I'd get in the way with my old ideas; but I can't help thinking they're better ideas. Like, I have names for the cows, not numbers which is what the EC is all about.

'Farming used to be a sociable thing. At harvest-time, for example, we'd press the apples and have cider – my brother would come round and my friends, and we'd all help each other and we'd drink and talk in the fields, laugh and chat about everything. It isn't good now the way farming is carried on and I don't want to be part of it; perhaps that's why I've changed so little. People convince themselves it was all harder in the past with horses and carts and no tractors because they want to believe everything's all right now; but they know it isn't. Farming is easier, but it's worse because the life has gone out of it. Take the grass, for instance: great big mowing machines came down here with the incomers and they cut too much and killed all the lanes; and they killed all the wild pheasants and partridges in the fields because they cut twice a year. It was all just greed, factory boys on the land.

'We had the time to stop every now and then, but not any more. It's all rushing now, and making money. When I was young, if one farmer killed a lamb or a pig he'd share it with the other farmers round about; and we'd sell our butter and cream in Chagford. Now, of course, we're not allowed to sell a thing. And because of all these subsidies there are now only two cow farmers left in the Chagford area, and I'm one of them. 'Tis all wrong. People always wanted our cream for their children and at Easter – they were the great times for cream. Otherwise we fed a lot of it to the pigs. And then we'd have the pig at Christmas! We supplied the big houses, too, the gentry. It's the last ten years that have seen the biggest and the worse changes; now, for example, I've got to register every single animal, and I've got to clip the cows' ears and all sorts.'

But for Joe himself things have changed little over the decades, and if anything, he travels even less now than he did as a young man. 'Well, I used to ride the pony to school as a child, and I suppose that was a bit of travelling,' he says with a smile. 'Every day I'd get up on her and trot along the lanes, though really there wasn't anything special about that, because it was how everyone got around, or in a cart. And our pleasures were all here, too, either in the fields after harvest or in the barn if it was raining; we'd have cider and we'd kill our own pigs and chickens, not the London way, I know, but how my family have done things for generations; and I don't see no reason to change it all now.'

We moved on round the farm and up the deep overgrown lane, thick with foxgloves. Joe loves the countryside in and around the farm, but he is not sentimental about it; he remembers the pig killer calling each year until very recently, and wringing the necks of chickens was an everyday occurrence, their feathers used in pillows and bolsters. A lack of sentimentality does not mean, however, that he has anything of the cynic about him. He leaves cynicism to the modern farmers, those who believe that working the land is purely and simply a business, a way to make money; as he explains:

'I could make the fields bigger and get the combine in, and bother with all this EC nonsense, but why – to give me more leisure time? Leisure time for what? For going round causing trouble? No, I'm happy here doing what I've always done – or at least I was till this EC thing. I can't understand it at all. I can't take my eggs into Chagford any more to sell them; nor my milk, nor anything. I have to have my cows' ears nicked and tagged and

The southwest has always been famous for its cider

The Batworthy chaff-cutter

marked, and now I have to tell people in another country exactly what every square inch of the farm grows or is used for. It's a load of nonsense; and when I filled in the forms they even told me I hadn't got the acreage right!

'As good as the day it was made,' said Joe, suddenly changing the subject; we had moved out of the sunshine into another old granite building where a chaff cutter with its great curving handle stood oiled and ready for use, as if the thirty years since it was last regularly employed had dropped away in an instant. And the roller that bruised the corn for the horses was still there, too. 'All this stuff's been here since the day I first remember anything on this farm, and my father had them a long time before he even thought of me. We last used the chaff cutter for the last horse we had in the 1960s.

Father and I used to plough together, and before that an old boy called Frank Long worked for us, drove our horses till my brother and I were old enough. You could plough about one acre a day, which was more than enough on a small farm, and it was a lovely skilled and satisfying business when you got it right. You'd mark your line, and it was a matter of pride to get as straight a furrow as you could. We used to help the major who farmed nearby with his ploughing, too. I had two brothers and Annie, my sister, and we all worked then; I can still clearly

remember the fun we had in the cornfield at harvest-time as the last bit of it was cut and the rabbits came pouring out. They were everywhere, dozens of them, hundreds sometimes – the dogs used to chase them, and the children, everyone! But there are fewer rabbits now, myxy has seen to that, and we have less corn.

'We always kept two plough horses and another one for odd work, for pulling the mangel cart and suchlike, and Father always had something decent to ride; he liked to ride, and used the horse to go about selling potatoes, and he could always stop at the pubs because they all had stables for travellers and their horses.

'I remember at harvest-time how we all helped make the ricks, and that was a real skill; but we enjoyed helping, and eating and drinking, too, in the fields as we did the work. So many farms have those big machines now that make a great roll of hay

Relaxing at the end of a hard day

Corn ricks on the southern slopes of Dartmoor

all wrapped in plastic at the touch of a button. And when we were older and the days were wet we'd sit and drink cider and talk. You'd sit with all your mates and just chat about this and that. I don't know why we enjoyed it all so much, but we did. Of course there were arguments, too, like boundaries for example – there'd be terrible rows about them, and if you put a ferret down another man's hedgerow he'd shoot you if he could!'

If Joe seems against everything that has come into farming in the past twenty or thirty years it is only because he considers that the changes damage the local nature of his work, rooted as it is in the neighbourhood of Devon. He cannot accept, and many would sympathise with his view, that rules created in Brussels to cover farms in a dozen countries and in a thousand different locations, can be a better answer than solutions and farming practices worked out locally over centuries. For Joe, a Europe he neither knows nor cares much for, is telling him how to run a farm that he knows better than anyone in the world; and of course it goes against the grain. He can understand that during the last war it was essential that the country pull together to grow as much corn as possible – as a result he ploughed up his pastures as instructed – but he knew that the war would end, and that he could then return his land to its traditional use as pasture. Now he receives complex, unfathomable letters written in a style which refers to farming as though it were simply an industrial process of yields and averages, profit and loss, input and output; the distance from which the commands come and the inexplicable nature of their message strikes Joe as profoundly undemocratic.

Both Joe and Annie know that when they are gone the farm is likely to go to more incomers, and that, in a very real sense, they are the last link in a chain that stretches back, in essence unchanged, to medieval times; to days when the countryside was still populated by people who worked the land and did not commute to the nearest town to work in office and factory.

'Oh, we know it will all change,' says Joe 'but at least we won't be here to see it.'

'They give prizes for the biggest onions…'

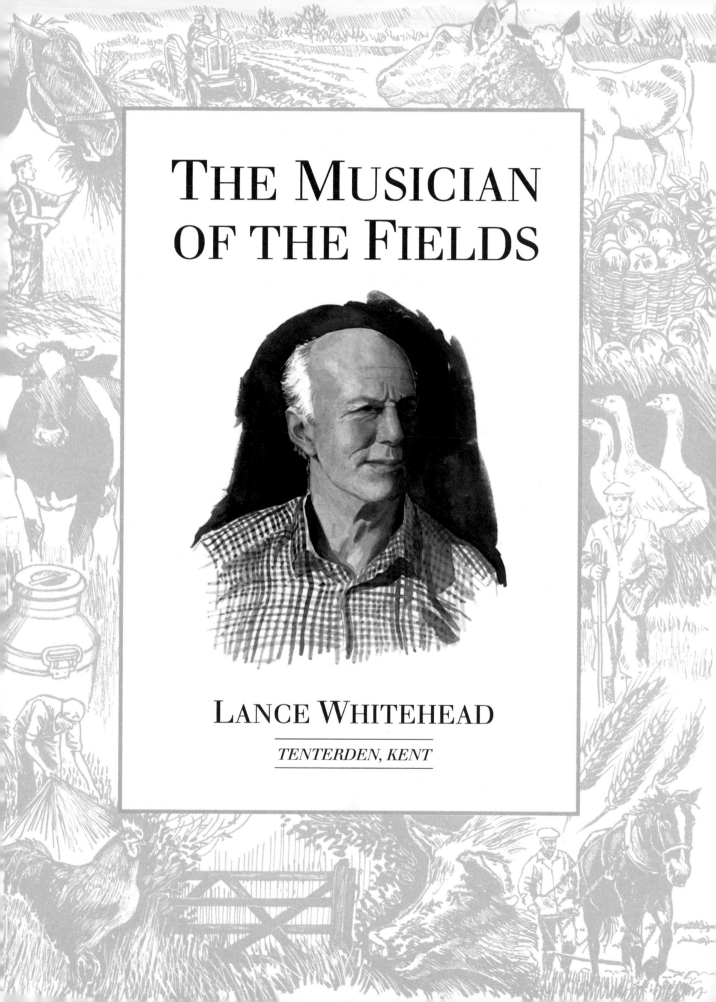

THE MUSICIAN
OF THE FIELDS

LANCE WHITEHEAD

TENTERDEN, KENT

Lance Whitehead, a surprisingly young-looking sixty-seven, sits in his massive beamed sitting-room and talks naturally and unprompted about a farming life that is probably as close to the old ways as it is possible to be today. He cuts his own wood for his fires in winter, tends his cattle and has no interest at all in agribusiness or in making money for the sake of it.

His house is a perfect example of a medieval hall house converted during Tudor times to a house with two floors, and it has hardly been touched in three hundred years. It has no damp course, and the baked floor-tiles in the sitting room are laid straight onto the sand; but none of this bothers him. 'Well, the floors do sweat a bit in winter, I must admit, and rain comes down the chimney, but it's warm enough so long as we burn a couple of wheelbarrow loads of logs each day!'

Lance laughs, and rocks back in his chair which, like all the other chairs in his sitting-room, is loaded with bits and pieces of wooden furniture designed to keep his black Labrador out of them. He throws another massive log – more like half a tree – on the fire, gently clouts the dog, and then goes on to tell me more about his father and his long line of Kentish ancestors: 'My family first came to this house in 1942, though I was born in a tiny cottage about half a mile away, one of a number of cottages bought by my grandfather who owned the windmill at the top of the lane. The windmill was burned down in 1913, and afterwards my father bought what remained of it together with the bakehouse, the grounds and some cottages.

'When my parents got married my grandfather gave them a cottage – he was a baker, originally at a place called Wittersham about three miles from here, but my grandmother

Lance aged about 17, with Jo and (right) working on the 5 November bonfire in the late forties

was a farmer's daughter from Biddenden, about four miles away; her family had farmed there for more than two hundred years. However, the house I live in now was built, we think, in about 1480; it is immensely higgledy-piggledy and is built entirely of oak timbers. I've lived here for fifty years.' Forstall Farm stands alone at the end of a long lane. Pasture runs almost to the door, and the house has views over the Weald that can have changed little in this peaceful corner of Kent for centuries. Lance is particularly conscious of farming as a way of life, and in his case, a way of life that goes back for generations:

'My wife's grandfather was a hop grower, but she came from a long line of farmers going back centuries.

My parents moved into this ancient house on 11 October 1942, Michaelmas Day – everything in those days was sorted out, or let or rented either from Michaelmas Day or from Lady Day in March. If you went into a farm you always started at Lady Day, and you had to buy the farm and also its valuation, by which was meant the value of the work and effort already put into it, the crops already growing, the hedges laid, the fences and so on. You would judge what had been done by walking around and looking at the state of things generally.

'Every year now you have to do the same thing for the taxman, so if you keep a few more cows you have to declare it so he can take his cut. We used to have a professional valuer in each year, but now I do it all myself.

'I was eleven when we moved here, and though Mum came from farming stock, Dad was a Londoner really. He'd been injured in the Great War and his brother had been killed; when he came back to England to recuperate he was sent down to a farm. A lot of people did the same – the appeal of good country air, I suppose – and obviously they thought that would be best for a while; but Dad must have really enjoyed it because he never went back to London. He worked on several farms, and eventually became what was known as a milk recorder; in fact he was the first one in Kent.

'Well, this job as milk recorder meant that instead of continuing as a herdsman, which is what he'd done first when he came down to Kent, he had to cycle all over the county recruiting farmers to this sort of co-operative; the idea was the fore-runner of the Milk Marketing Board. However he gave it up in March 1923 and then worked for a cattle feed merchant. He was what was known then as a commission agent, that is he would go round and sell cattle, pig and poultry feed using the contacts he'd made when he'd worked as a milk recorder.'

Lance's father made a great success of this work, but World War II put paid to it because the War Department decided that all feedstuff manufacturers should be nationalised. 'I suppose it was inevitable,' says Lance with a wry smile, 'because everything was in short supply, but for us it meant that my father was out of a job. He looked around to see what he could do and decided that, as he'd been working as a special constable, he should try being a regular cop. So he had a chequered career – but what all this is really leading up to is his decision to come here.

'There's a Forstall Farm in virtually every area of Kent, and I think the word means a place where things are bought and sold, a sort of unofficial market place. I think it comes from the word 'fostte' which was a place where you could buy and sell without going into the town and paying a toll at the gates.

'Anyway, the tenancy of this place came up because the couple who were farming it at the start of the second war were very old and just couldn't carry on. Lots of farms were still derelict at that time – it was particularly bad between the wars right across Britain. The War Agricultural Commission was empowered to have any ground they chose ploughed up for the war effort, and the order came through to this old couple to plough up the Big Field. They said it couldn't be done because it was in such a mess with thistles, anthills and so on; they had come to the farm in 1897 and the Big Field hadn't been ploughed in living memory. It was twenty-six acres of rough ground, although maps from 1860 show it was then split into four fields, but Mum and Dad were determined to do it when they came, so they got hold of a thing called a D2 – it was like a tank! An ordinary tractor couldn't have done the job. Some farmers had the old Fordson tractors in those days; the first Fordson was built just before the Great War, but it wasn't updated till 1944 and even then the updated model had only three gears. Anyway, we used the D2, and we got the Big Field ploughed; but even with that great tank of a thing it was tough going.

'All the mowers and binders and reaping machines were powered then by the movement of their own wheels – modern equipment has power for the wheels *and* power for the binder or whatever it is – so if the wheels slipped on the ground you lost power. These early machines were pulled by horses, too, so there wasn't much traction, and hence power, anyway. They were odd-looking things, too, with drive belts running all over the place.'

But even in the late 1930s and early 1940s much farm-work in Lance's part of Kent was still done by hand or with the help of horses. 'It wasn't *most* of the work here, it was *all* the work, or that's how it seemed. And it was only when the War Office created machinery depots that things began to change because only then could more farmers use machines and get over their long-standing prejudice against anything new-fangled.'

66

By today's standards, of course, the early pieces of mechanical agricultural equipment seem positively antedeluvian, but for farmers like Lance they represented some relief from back-breaking physical labour. 'The old binders were useful but very unwieldy. They had a six-foot wide cut and were too big to go straight through a field gate; they had to be towed through sideways. A winding handle lowered the driving wheel once the thing was in position, and when you did this the wheels on which it ran were lifted off the ground; thus

Pasture runs almost to the door . . . Forstall Farm, where little has changed for centuries

the machine stayed still, and we brought the corn to it. I remember when it first arrived it took us all day to work out how to set it up and use it! A big cog on the driving wheel to the main chain drove the blades and sweeps and the hay was lifted onto a canvas conveyer, then lifted onto an elevator over the driving mechanism to the other side where it was packed into sheaves. Finally a knotter was activated. The whole thing was adjustable and you set the height according to the height of the crop. Unlike a modern combine harvester, the one we used seemed to involve men everywhere, operating levers or rushing about adjusting things.

'Before the old binders could be set going the field still had to be "opened up" by hand: a man would scythe a wide path right round the field and only then did the tractor have enough room to tow the machine round the field to harvest the rest of the crop. Like most of the smaller farms, we couldn't afford to buy a machine so we hired one each year at harvest time.'

Lance's parents (centre) with Heinz May (left) and Arno Striegler (right), German POW's. (Top right) Ma and Heinz May, with a sow, in 1948. (Right) Heinz and John loading sheaves at harvest time

But if agriculture had become easier just after the end of the second war, family life for Lance was about to take a more difficult turn. 'My father just walked out one day when my brother and I were in our late teens; he just disappeared for good and we haven't seen him since. But my mother decided to carry on with the farm, and as luck would have it, this being just after the war, she had two German prisoners of war to help. Like most prisoners who were sent onto the farms, our two were very hard-working; many stayed on for good when the war ended, and although one of ours went back to his home in 1946, the other, Heinrich, stayed on until he died in 1992.

'In 1950, three years after my father disappeared, my brother and I decided to take on the farm. We didn't really know much about running a farm, although of course we'd worked for Mother for years during school and college holidays. I still felt slightly the amateur, I suppose, because I could have had another career as a musician.' In fact Lance had studied at the Guildhall School of Music in London for a number of years. However, the pull of the land had been too strong; he disliked living in London, and was much happier back farming where science and technology were making further inroads.

'One of the great things in the late 1940s and early 1950s was the elimination of TB in herds of dairy cattle. Our cows were OK, so we decided to register the herd as an attested TB-free herd; this was an expensive thing to do, but it meant we would be able to get more for our milk. Then everything went wrong: Mother bought a cow that seemed fine, but it died, and then the others died – they all died eventually, and it was heartbreaking. There and then we decided we would no longer buy in cows as the risk was too great. We still get occasional problems with them, but if they close you down these days because the herd is infected, at least you get compensation.'

Like most farmers, Lance and his brother ran Forstall as a mixed farm, thus minimising the risk of overall loss should any particular enterprise suddenly drop disastrously in value in years of general over-production. 'When we first took over, my brother and I kept pigs and poultry as well as cattle, and we grew corn.

'All our hay was turned by hand in those days. We raked it into rows having cut it using our old Fordson tractor and a converted horse mower, and eventually built it into a rick; and that *was* a very skilled business. First we'd put faggots – bundles of sticks – on the ground to keep the hay up off the damp soil. Then we'd work round a central pile of hay which was always kept higher than the outside edge, and gradually it would rise from the ground. The idea was to keep the rick slightly domed so the rain would run off quickly; and the theory is that each pitch of hay holds down the one below.'

That was the theory, but as Lance laughingly confessed, things didn't always go as planned and in truth a wayward hayrick could be a terror: 'We had some disasters –

sometimes the rick would seem fine until you'd nearly finished it, and then almost without warning, the whole lot would begin to lean and you were in real trouble! You could prop it up if you were lucky, but one of the effects of its great weight was to exacerbate hugely any tendency to lean one way or another – and once it had started to lean it might very suddenly all avalanche into a great untidy pile. But I'm sure it happened now and then to the best of farmers.

'Sometimes when we piled the hay on the waggon it was just as bad; waggon-loads of hay weren't always those neat things you see in paintings, and you might have to pull the cart back to the rick-yard with a couple of men holding the hay in with sticks from one side. Once the rick was built, it would be given a proper thatched roof just like a house roof. The weight of hay on hay meant it would end up packed very tight, which is why chunks had to be cut out with a special hay knife. With re-seeded hay you have hollow stems, too, so after a few weeks all the hollow would be crushed out of it in the rick, and what had been ten or twelve feet high would have sunk to head height.

'When my brother and I first started here we had only a couple of house cows which supplied just our needs, but eventually we had ten or twelve milking cows and we could make a reasonable living from their milk. At one time early on we survived by selling the milk from just four cows, real subsistence stuff! It was hard work milking then, even with only a few animals, because you had to milk by hand at least twice a day and sometimes three times if you wanted the maximum yield of milk. We'd put the milk in churns and take them up to the end of the lane where they were collected by the milk lorry. It's all much easier now with tankers and sterile tanks and so on. We got our first milking machine in 1952 – it cost £150, and it's the only thing I've ever had on hire purchase! Forty years later we're still using bits and pieces of that original machine.

'We used to get up at 6am, which wasn't really early by farming standards, and one of us would milk the cows while the other fed the calves and pigs. Then we'd go into the house for breakfast before getting out again to clean out the cowshed. If it was haymaking time we'd perhaps spend the morning turning a piece that had been mowed; we eventually stopped doing it by hand when we bought a hay-turning machine for £5! This was just a couple of wheels and a series of rakes that moved to one side and flipped the hay over – you had to turn the hay like this in the field to make sure it was dry before you took it to be ricked. Balers were only just starting to appear at this time.

'Most of our corn was grown for the cattle, though we also grew oats and beans. We kept the straw for bedding. My brother did most of the ploughing and harrowing, and then we'd both do the hoeing which was incredibly back-breaking work in the days before weedkillers – my back has never been the same since. All the planting we did by hand, and we sowed by hand, too, using a box with two handles and an iron wheel; as you pushed it along it popped the seeds out. But it was such slow, laborious work that in the end we just couldn't cope with it. All farm-work then was laborious, though. Another job we had to do every day was to make a huge pile of mangels and pulp them by hand which we then mixed with chaff and oats to feed to the cattle; they absolutely loved it, though now they get cattle cake that we buy in, and hay. Again, it just makes the work less hard for the farmer.'

Lance has happy memories of family harvests, and even in winter, farming with his brother was a sociable business – 'you're a bit lonely in one of those air-conditioned modern tractor cabs' he says – but it was very much a 24-hour a day job, with few breaks and holidays. 'There were so many things to be done in a day. Just take weeds, for example. Weeds were a terrible headache for all farmers forty or more years ago, particularly if you let them get ahead of you. That first crop we grew on the Big Field was supposed to be wheat, but it turned out to be a crop of hay, wheat and weeds in equal measure!

'Weeds were particularly bad in this area – we used to say that we were still picking thistles out of our shins at Christmas. But although I complain about the weeds I suppose it has to be said that along with the weeds there were more wild flowers around, and thicker hedges; the countryside was very different. When I was young I loved the rooks, too, although the farmers thought there were too many of them. That sound was the sound of my boyhood, and flocks were so big you'd see them flying by for half an hour. On windy autumn days we used to watch them as they battled their way through the headwinds. They were certainly a hell of a nuisance on beans, but they ate a lot of pests too, wireworms and so on. There are far fewer now.'

Forstall Farm extends to 104 acres, of which 25 are woodland; because the woodland isn't all in one place – 'it sort of splits the land up' says Lance – farming it is difficult: there are ten acres of wood roughly in the middle of the farm, another smaller wood circles a field, and there's a band of trees on the southern boundary '. . . more a strip really, just a few yards wide,' says Lance. On the other hand, Lance has always had enough fuel for the enormous fires in the house.

If on the whole the woodland was seen as an asset, rabbits were certainly not. 'Oh, rabbits were terrible here before the coming of myxomatosis. The old couple who had the farm before we came said they lived almost entirely on rabbits. They were a cheap food for many country people, but because you could have them all the time and they were associated with the poor, most people didn't want to eat them; they just wanted to be rid

of them. After myxy the farm was clear of rabbits for years, and we saw grass for the first time; in the pre-myxy days the rabbits would clear a field in hours – in the morning you could look out over fields that were bare that had been green the night before.

'During the war rabbits were considered so bad that the War Committee set up teams of trappers; they used gins, which are now illegal because they are so cruel, but they were very effective. The team sent down here once caught five hundred rabbits in a week, though that was probably because before the war the farm was virtually derelict and the rabbits had had a real chance to get ahead. At that time the agent said to us that Mr Holmewood, the previous tenant, managed to starve half a sheep to the acre! That's how difficult a farm it was seen to be.'

But it was for precisely this reason – a difficult farm on relatively poor soil – that it was at least cheap to rent. 'We got it for just £1 per acre, though Dad was the only person prepared to pay anything at all to take it on. Most people wouldn't have looked at it rent free!'

There was little money to be made in those early years, but at least Lance and his brother were independent; and things were so bad that it was widely assumed they couldn't get worse. Also, they were allowed access to better pastures through an ancient system of grazing rights, whereby Forstall animals could be summered on distant ground. 'Lots of farms hereabouts had what they called fattening ground down on Romney Marsh, and could put their bullocks down there to fatten up during the summer. We couldn't produce the quality of the grass they had down there, and it suited the marsh farmers because we paid them for the right to graze their land.'

Although it was never likely to make them rich, Forstall was a farm that Lance knew well; he also knew that it would at least always provide him with an adequate living; so when at last the chance came to buy it, he felt little hesitation. 'We didn't buy until 1953, and the farm had belonged to a Quaker family for centuries. We dealt with two sisters originally, Margaret and Anne Fry, though in fact before we took it on they had intended it to go to the National Trust largely because the house is so remarkable and unspoiled. When we first came as tenants even the massive, centuries-old bread oven was still here, built up against one end of the house; but we got permission from the agent to take it out, together with an old copper – it must have been hundreds of years old and would, I suppose, be a real rarity now, but it wasn't much use to us, and in those days things weren't considered interesting in the way they are now. However, that wasn't the way one of the sisters saw it: she thought the bread oven was a real feature, and because she wanted the house to go to the National Trust, when she discovered it had been removed the agent got a real dressing-down. Miss Fry considered we'd destroyed an important feature of the house, and I suppose we had.

72

'Eventually an official from the National Trust did come to look at the house, but they didn't want it, largely, I think, because it needed to have so much money spent on it. And when she found that the Trust wasn't interested in it, Miss Fry sold it to us. It was valued at £1,000 as an investment, although the valuer said that if it was sold to the tenant – ourselves, that is – a fair price would be £1,500; but Miss Fry had always had a certain sympathy for my mother's plight, so she sold it to us for £1,000. She wasn't really interested in money, so much so that she even lent us the money to buy it from her!

'Both Margaret and Anne Fry are long dead; they were unmarried and lived in London, and other than that I know nothing about them, except that they were certainly marvellous landlords. Three years before she sold the house to us, Miss Fry had a cowshed built for us which cost more than the house was worth!'

The small-scale nature of Forstall Farm is unusual today – 'We definitely count as small fry!' says Lance – but even so, the days when a farmer and his family could keep going on the income from a few cows are long gone. 'To make a good living these days you really need at least sixty cows. I have forty, and a few beef cattle. It wasn't always so, but with the rise in agribusiness and so on we are now classed as a small farm, which is how I like it. We could increase the herd to fifty, I suppose, but bits of the farm are difficult to get to. Cows are certainly my main interest these days. I've been making my living more or less solely with cows since 1950, even though in this part of Kent traditionally hops were grown; but there was little money in hops until the Hop Marketing Board started – certainly terrible trouble to make a living growing them. I think the last hops were grown around here in the 1920s, and in fact hop growing is in decline all over Kent now because new varieties of beer are lighter so the demand for hops has decreased.'

The life of the small farmer is almost invariably a quiet one. He has his animals to feed and his crops to tend; the hours are long, and as the numbers of farm-workers have declined the farmer's life has increasingly become one of solitude. However, Lance does have hobbies and interests that take him away, however temporarily, from his secluded life:

'My great hobby has always been shooting, and we used to have great days before myxomatosis. Ours were nothing like the Edwardian days on the grand shoots where they'd say about a duck or a pheasant "Up goes a guinea, bang goes a penny and down comes half a crown!" – we just used to get together with all the farmers round about for vermin shoots, rabbits, jays, magpies and so on; it was our bit of fun and way of socialising, because it's very difficult for a farmer to take a holiday, as you can imagine. I did try it once or twice but it doesn't work well. You have to get someone in to do the work, but he won't know your animals, won't know what each animal is fed, and when and how, so you have to give him a list of what needs doing and it's all very hit and miss. You worry when you're away, and usually you have to sort it all out when you get back!'

The solitude of farming increased for Lance when, quite amicably, he parted from his brother in the early 1950s. 'When my brother married we knew the farm couldn't manage all of us, so I bought him out. He farms on the Isle of Wight now, but my son Bruce helps me and will eventually take over the farm. He's at the Royal Agricultural College at Cirencester, but mucks in during the holidays. Yes, he'll certainly take over unless things get very bad. Things are always difficult on a small, traditionally run place like this, with not a great deal of land and only a few animals. When he comes back to work with me full time and not just in the college vacations, I don't quite know how I'll be able to pay him a living wage, because it's really only a one-man band. Still, I'm sure we'll manage.

'My other son, Giles, is an artist, and my daughter Tabitha, who's sixteen, still goes to school. She walks two miles each day into Tenterden which is the nearest town, but she helps around the place when she can. I suppose I'm one of the few remaining subsistence farmers in the sense that I see it as a way of life; a way to make a living. I don't see it as a business in the way that many bigger farmers do.

'My wife was heavily involved in farming; she was originally from Sheffield, and she died in 1990. She was captain of the Tenterden bellringers before she married me! I suppose we had music in common – I still play the cello, in two local orchestras at Cranbrook and Hastings. And two nights a week every week, and one additional night I play in a string quartet. So there's plenty to do and I'm kept out of harm's way!'

Lance doesn't regret the road he took in life, despite the fact that he could easily have opted for the life of a musician. 'My cello teacher studied with Pablo Casals so I was well taught, but my first love has always been the farm, which diversified a bit when my wife decided to breed Labradors – they were very good, too, and she used to sell them all over the world. They won lots of prizes in field trials and so on.

'But just to go back to shooting for a minute, I should say that I started with Dad who used to go out every Tuesday after Ashford Market. My very earliest memories are the smell of a wet dog and of Dad cleaning his gun in the evening.'

Lance keeps only Guernsey cows today, because milk is paid for on the basis of its quality and Guernsey milk is very high quality indeed. Gone are the days when all milk was paid for at a flat rate regardless of quality; although, as Lance explains, other than keeping the right animals, there isn't much you can do about it: 'The quality of your milk depends to a large extent on the sort of land you've got – in other words, it

depends on the soil. After decades of spreading dung on our land we've improved it a great deal, and it is now very good quality, producing marvellous grass; but it wasn't like that when we first came. We're on what's known as Wadhurst clay here, but we're only just on it, and in fact it isn't *that* good anyway unless it's well looked after, as we've looked after it. It's a sort of marginal area almost on the marsh – Romney Marsh, that is.

'I should say that our woods are difficult to coppice here, too, because much of the woodland grows in steep gills; but we still cut our own firewood and we have plenty of chestnut for fence-posts. Chestnut is marvellous, and will last for twenty years or more even if the ground is wet. It also makes wonderful roof timbers. Ash and hornbeam, by contrast, will rot in the ground in a year.'

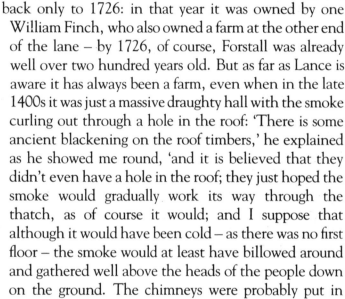

Lance has a long list of the people who farmed at Forstall before his family arrived, but in spite of its length the list encompasses merely a third of the life of the farm, going back only to 1726: in that year it was owned by one William Finch, who also owned a farm at the other end of the lane – by 1726, of course, Forstall was already well over two hundred years old. But as far as Lance is aware it has always been a farm, even when in the late 1400s it was just a massive draughty hall with the smoke curling out through a hole in the roof: 'There is some ancient blackening on the roof timbers,' he explained as he showed me round, 'and it is believed that they didn't even have a hole in the roof; they just hoped the smoke would gradually work its way through the thatch, as of course it would; and I suppose that although it would have been cold – as there was no first floor – the smoke would at least have billowed around and gathered well above the heads of the people down on the ground. The chimneys were probably put in when the first floor was added, perhaps a hundred years after the hall was built.'

I followed Lance up the massive oak staircase, with its treads of solid carved triangular pieces of oak, and across the ancient floors, through rooms that seem to double back on themselves. Then suddenly we were descending another staircase in a completely different part of the house. There is hardly a straight wall to be found anywhere, but the massive wall and roof beams have survived the test of time; and if all goes well Forstall Farm is likely to look out over the Kentish Weald for many centuries yet.

For Clipping of Sheepe

CLIPPERS are to have 4d a score. Then are you to send them about noon a groates worth of ale and bread and cheese and perhaps a cheesecake and against that time they make an end you are to make ready a dinner for them.

Clippers bring usually two pairs of sheares; you are to give charge to them that they have an especial care of prickinge the skin; wherefore you are to always have a dish standing by either with tar or sheep salve, that if they chance to give a little clippe you may lay tar on it and there is no further danger.

There is 6d allowed to a piper for playing to the clippers all the day.

The Farming and Account Books of Henry Best of Helmswell, 1641

Falling Prices

AT Chertsey where we came into Surrey again, there was a fair for horses, cattle and pigs. I did not see any sheep. Everything was exceedingly dull. Cart colts, two and three years old, were selling for less than a third of what they sold for in 1813.

The cattle were of an inferior description to be sure; but the price was low almost beyond belief. Cows, which would have sold for 15 shillings in 1813 did not get buyers at 3 shillings. I had not time to enquire much about the pigs, but a man told me that they were dirt cheap.

William Cobbett, *Rural Rides,* 1830

For Buying and Selling Butter

BUTTER is either bought and sold by the pound or the cake and in every cake there is 2lb; in the beginning of Lent we pay 10d a cake, about the 20th of April 3d a pound and then about the middle of May it will fall to 2d and 2 quarters a pound; then it is at the cheapest.

If we chance to want in Lent time we furnish ourselves either at Beverley or Malton Market, which country folkes bring thitherto to sell, but the best buying is at Beverley. When we intend that our foreman shall buy butter we have him out a maunde and a cloathe the night before. I have knowne us buy and spend constantly, tenne and twelve pound of butter in the week.

The Farming and Account Books of Henry Best of Helmswell, 1641

Two-way Traffic

STRAW was a basic necessity for livestock farming, providing litter for animals kept in stalls, sties or cattle courts; oats, hay and straw were also sold for the stables in the towns from which dung was returned by cart and railway to the market towns in Hertfordshire, Bedfordshire, Kent, Sussex and Worcestershire.

But this double trade, fodder and straw moving from the farms into the towns and dung moving back, is threatened as the motor car and the motor lorry supplant the urban horse.

Agrarian History of England, 1934

Starting Young

AS a babe the first words he lisps are the names of the horses. Does he cry – he is taken to see Prince, or lifted up to pat Diamond. He no sooner learns to walk than he finds his way to the stables, toddling with the rest of the family after da da as he spends hour after hour baiting his charges.

Thus from earliest infancy he is receiving a technical education. He hears of nothing, thinks of nothing, but of that one business by which he is to live; the stable becomes playroom and schoolroom combined; all his ideas centre in it and gather round it and when in due course he becomes a mate, he displays at once an inborn and inbred faculty for managing horses.

Richard Heath, *The English Peasant,* 1893

Opium for the Masses

VIRTUALLY the only analgesic available in rural homes was an opium preparation of one kind or another; Godfrey's Cordial or Daffy's Elixir. The unhappy natives of the fens fill up their cup of misery by becoming opium eaters.

Every village has its own peculiar preparation ... the favourite form for infants being Godfrey's Cordial, a mixture of opium, treacle and sassafras. Each mother buys the Godfrey she favours most so that, when she leaves her baby in the morning, she will leave her bottle with the nurse. Should the nurse substitute her own and should it turn out more potent the children sink into such a state that, in a fright, the nurse sends off for the surgeon who, on his arrival, finds half a dozen babies, some snoring, some squinting, all pallid and eye-sunken, lying about the room.

Happily he is prepared for the emergency, applies the stomach pump and the poisoned infants come round.

Supposing they clear this danger and grow up, the habit thus induced often stays with them for life. It is well known that in no part of England is there such a quantity of this drug consumed as in the Fenland.

Wholesale druggists report that they send immense quantities into these districts, and retail druggists often dispense as much as 200 pounds a year. It is sold in pills or penny sticks, and a thriving shop will serve three or four hundred customers on a Saturday night, the largest consumers being the inhabitants of small hamlets or isolated cottages in the fens.

Richard Heath, *The English Peasant*, 1893

How to Choose a Good Tuppe

LET him be large and well quartered, of a snoode and a good stapple, with a long and bushy tail, without hornes and having both the stones in the codde; and lastly never under two sheare, nor seldom above five for being over young; their blood is hot and the scabbe procured and being over olde their radical moisture is wasted.

The Farming and Account Books of Henry Best of Helmswell, 1641

Worthless Fellows

FARMERS are often I think worthless fellows. Few lords will cheat and when they do they will be ashamed of it; farmers cheat and are not in the least ashamed. They have all the sensuous vices too of the nobility, with cheating into the bargain.

Boswell's Life of Samuel Johnson, 1790

For Selling of Corn

WE seldom send fewer than eight horse loads of corn to market, with them two men, for one man cannot guide the pokes of above four horses. On Wednesday when they go with oats to Beverley they put their horses into stables that are hard by the market place where there is hay ready for them against they go in; and there do they pay halpennies [sic] a piece for their horses for their hay and stable room. When our folkes go to Malton they are usually stirring about four hours before day which is about three of the clock and then will they be about Grimstone by the spring of the day and at Malton by 9 of the clock at the furthest; for in winter time that market is the quickest about 9 of the clock because the badgers come far many of them, wherefore their desire is to buy soon that they may be going betimes for feare of being nighted.

On market days our folkes give to every two horses one bottle of hay; so soon as their panniers are on and everything fitted they lead them forth and so many are tied together each in other's tail; then do they carry one company after another to the garner door and turning them about with their heads towards the gates all the fellows that are able to carry pokes fall to loading; they give every horse half his load before that any one be wholly laden.

Then one of the boys setteth open the broad gates and so soon as they are gotten out, shutteth them again. The other folkes go with them usually to the brick wall nook or lane end; then when they come back they fall to mucking of the stables.

The Farming and Account Books of Henry Best of Helmswell, 1641

Castle and Corn

I AM sure that it is easier to drive fat cattel one hundred miles than to carry corn forty on land. Neither would I have Chiltern ground turned to pasture because there an acre of arable is worth more than an acre of pasture. Yet certainly it plainly appears by this that generally there is more want of pasture in England than of arable, for that we have daily fat cattel brought out of Ireland and Scotland, but never any go out, but where grain comes in once it goes out ten times.

George Atwell, *The Faithfull Surveyour*, 1663

At the Head of Swaledale

THE people here at the head of Swaledale are mainly shepherd farmers, working themselves, assisted perhaps by a couple of men who live in the house, and eat and drink with them. If these men get married they live out of the house, and receive about twelve or thirteen shillings a week, but they generally wait until they have saved a little money and can take a small farm and begin on their own account.

This is not difficult to do as every householder has a right of pasturage for their cattle and sheep on the moors from the 29th of May until winter. During the winter the cattle are shut up in the cow byres and fed on hay, but the poor sheep have to do the best they can on the moor. This is a hard time for the shepherds as the roads get snowed up and the sheep in danger of being lost. However, they collect them in little places of refuge, resembling the Northumberland stells. Often the boys have to go out on the moors with great bundles of hay on their heads to feed the sheep.

During the summer time, about six o'clock every afternoon, the cow herds go out with great tin cases slung over their shoulders, uttering a shrill cry to call the cattle off the moors. Rarely have they any trouble for the cattle are so accustomed to the hour that they would return of themselves, even if there were no call.

The cottages are seldom on a level with the road standing either above or below it. I was invited into one which lay considerably below the roadside, inhabited by a couple who had evidently married late in life. Spotlessly clean was their parlour, chairs, table and floor, bright as hand polish and soap water could make them. There was the tall mahogany clock case, made at the time of the wedding.

There too was a shorter clock and a barometer. Dazzling was the burnished steel of the great fire range, notwithstanding the good fire which burned in the grate, though it was only August. From the ceiling hung suspended long planks of cedar wood whereon they stowed away their oatmeal cakes and other commodities. Instead of pictures the walls were ornamented with numerous mourning cards framed and glazed.

They placed me in a great rocking chair, and while the farmer sat opposite me in another, the good wife fetched a glass of milk and some oatcake.

The farmer thought things wonderfully improved in the dale since his childhood; hardly any land was then enclosed, all was open moor. For even these quiet spots see great changes. The tide of humanity is forever ebbing and flowing. Thus twelve hundred years ago, the Swale must have had a vast population on its banks if it be true that Paulinus baptised 10,000 converts in its waters.

Now human beings are so scarce that a visitor is a curiosity. Immediately I entered the village the news was transmitted to the minister that a 'stranger in mannerly claes had come to Keld'.

Richard Heath, *The English Peasant*, 1893

A Light at Night

I WILL show you how to keep fire a long while light with a little charge. Suppose you dwell in a lone farmhouse, where one is sick and you have but one farthing candle in the house and borrow you cannot and you would fain have it burn a whole long winter's night; then do thus. Cut your candle in two pieces, light one of them; heat a great pin and thrust it into the great end of the candle long-wise half the pin's length. Then fill a pail of water so deep that the candle, pin and all, will not reach bottom. Let it down into the water till it comes to the flame, there staying it awhile till the water be still; then take away your hand so still as it burns the water will raise it and which answers the whole business that the fire will go no otherways save upward to his own element.

George Atwell, *The Faithfull Surveyour*, 1663

A MARSHMAN, BORN AND BRED

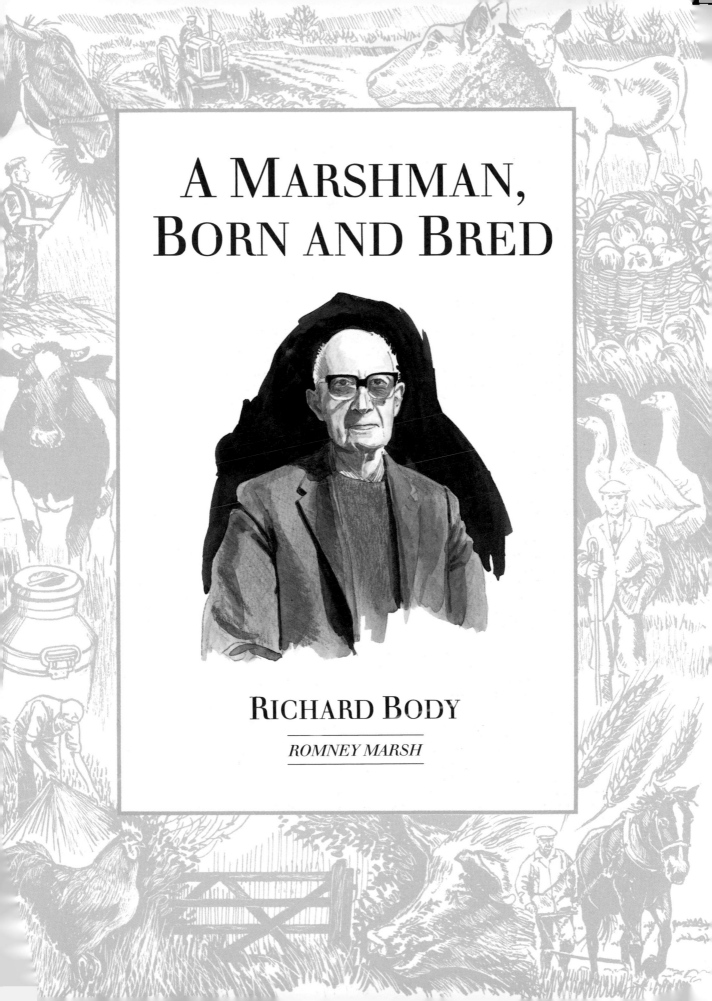

RICHARD BODY

ROMNEY MARSH

'When I was young, before the Great War, we mostly grew peas, long-pod beans and turnip seed for the seed merchants. This was an excellent area for that sort of thing, along with a small part of Essex and a great deal of Lincolnshire, the reason being that each of these areas has less than the normal amount of rainfall. Turnips and beans were all sown by hand then, and it was very hard work, I can tell you. And of course we didn't have the chemicals and sprays that are used today – in fact we weren't so active at all when it came to pests; we just accepted that they were there and treated them as best we could, but we were only able to use the techniques we'd inherited from our forefathers.'

Richard Body is an old man now, but he is tall, straight and courteous in a delightfully old-fashioned way. His farm, Hope Farm, lies on the very edge of that most haunting part of England, Romney Marsh, down at the southernmost tip of Kent and just a few miles from the ancient unspoiled towns of Rye and Winchelsea, towns virtually untouched by modern development. He is ninety-one now, but he remembers with the utmost clarity growing up on a remote marsh farm; and as he proudly declares, he was almost born on the marsh, something which has a special meaning for him and others like him:

'The marsh is like no other place in Britain. It has its own traditions and ways, and at one time it had a lot of words of its own, almost its own language. I grew up at St Mary's and I still have the letter my grandfather wrote, offering £30 a year for 300 acres of arable land in the parish. Then another letter written soon after explained that money was rather tight and withdrew the offer – my grandfather was a shrewd man! It took two more years before the family finally took the farm in 1898.'

Richard is a keen historian of local affairs, though as he explains, much of the history both of his family and of the marsh has been handed down by word of mouth. But the Bodys have certainly been farmers for generations: 'My aunt told me that the Body family came originally from Cornwall, probably early in the 1700s; and I've been able to trace the family back to 1780, to East Sussex. Though we were mostly farmers there is a record, from about 1715, of a Body from Westfield just outside Hastings and a direct ancestor of mine, who was apprenticed to a clockmaker. The family moved from East Sussex into Kent some time in the nineteenth century, to the Isle of Oxley and to Wittersham where distant members of the family live to this day. Most of the Bodys have left farming now; only my family and that of a cousin are still on the land.'

Much of the land on the edge of the marsh was originally allowed to flood in winter to help provide early grass for farmers further inland, for their summer grazing; the marsh farmers still call these men hill farmers. The latter would hire men to look after their cattle and sheep, and shepherds in the area are still called lookers by the local people; in the old days the lookers were paid so much an acre per year.

Hope Farm, where Richard now lives in semi-retirement, is on the old sea wall, far inland from the present main sea defence. However, over the centuries floods and storms have caused shifts in the sea defences, and even in the course of the local rivers: 'Originally the River Rother reached the sea near Hythe,' he explains, 'but it silted up and was diverted to reach the sea at Romney. Then in the thirteenth century a massive storm upset everything and the course of the river returned to Rye. There have been so many

The Body family at Gibbet Farm in 1907. Richard is standing second from the left in the front row

changes to the area over the centuries; and *millions* of years ago mile upon mile of forest grew here. Now and then we still plough up the fossilised trunks of the trees buried in the peat.

'I was born in 1904, at the farm my grandfather had taken over at St Mary's and which my father managed from about 1900. I've still got a list of the prices we paid for all the tackle we took over, the carts and waggons, drills and ploughs. None of that gear had changed much in centuries – a medieval farmer would have been quite happy to have used what we had!'

Richard has fond memories of those far-off days, but equally he has no illusions about them: 'Crops were dealt with in a totally different way in those days because everything was done by hand, and it was laborious. All crops were sold by the bushel, which was a measure of volume, not weight: this meant that when you filled a bag with corn you had to be careful about the way you did it – if you did it badly, the corn would sink too far into the bag and you'd have to put more in. There was a special skill in filling a bushel sack properly so that buyer and seller were happy that they'd exchanged a fair amount. If the corn was damp it had to be turned by hand to dry it, and that, like most farm jobs, was back-breaking work. When corn was threshed it was always by four-bushel sacks. Sacks were so important in those days that merchants and farmers who didn't have their own used to hire them from firms whose business it was to hire them out; there was, I recall, such a company up in London in Tooley Street called Starkie Room.

'If you sent Starkie a postcard on the Monday saying how many sacks you wanted, ton on the level. We also had a thatcher here full time and a stacker, for the haystacks.

'We had two rows of cottages where the farm-workers lived, and at Haffenden Farm, which my father bought in 1912, we tried to improve the workers' rooms which were in the attic. These had plastered walls and a partition to keep male and female workers apart, but not a single window. We put windows in, though by today's standards conditions were still pretty awful for both the house-servants and farm-workers.'

Richard is the first to admit that his family was luckier than most: 'The Bodys have always had money and land, though times have been difficult now and then' he says; much of this was inherited, in particular from his grandfather's wife for whom land was kept in trust until she was old enough to take it on. In their belief in the value of land, even during the difficult 1930s, the Bodys are typical of many ancient yeoman farmer families. And in his youth, Richard certainly knew ways and methods that his ancestors would have understood. 'Decisions were always made slowly and judgements were based on experience, not scientific measurement; for instance, a corn merchant in the old days would test a sample of corn by hand and by smell alone. These days they use machines to test for moisture content and all sorts.

'Before the Great War, little had changed for centuries. For example, I have a letter written about a Romney Marsh farmer in 1786, and the practices it describes are just the ones I remember, more or less. We still drove the sheep along the roads as they did then, though not quite so far. This is the writer's description of how the sheep went to market:

Soon after lambing is over they begin to draw off their old sheep that were set on to fattening the Michaelmas before. They are generally sent some in the wool, some out of the wool, as the season advances, to the London market, which is about 70 miles off, by Drovers who make that their employment. They are nearly a week in going, travelling at about the rate of 14 miles a day and are consigned to some particular salesman in Smithfield market. The salesman receives them off the drover at some place in the neighbourhood of London. He has them to the next market at Smithfield, two of which are held weekly, on Mondays and Fridays; he sells them to the carcase butchers and writes by that day's post to the owners informing them to whom he has sold them and at what price and deducting expenses of droving and selling which comes on the whole to about 1 / shilling a head. The grazier draws for the money which is paid at sight, so that he himself has no trouble whatever in the business. There are other smaller markets on this side of London called as the Lower Markets where they sometimes send their fatting sheep – ie Tunbridge, Maidstone and Rochester. In these markets the drovers are the salesmen who take and bring home the money to their employers and if any of the sheep tire on the road they sell and account for them.'

For Richard, records like this from the end of the eighteenth century are not much different from his own memories of life on the marsh early this century. 'If it was a real wet day the waggoner or his mate took the horses that needed shoeing to the forge where, of course, others would have gathered for the same reason; so there would be a queue and a long wait. I can remember the men standing in under the covered part of the building well out of the rain, but with their shoulders protected by sacking. They always enjoyed it because they could have a good old chat while they waited.

'Another important job for the waggoner was to grease all the waggon- and cart-wheels. This was normally a two-man job. The carts were great heavy things and each wheel had to be jacked up in turn. The linch-pin was then taken out with what we called a linch-pin drawer, a T-shaped tool with a claw that slid along the round, half-inch shaft. This claw hooked under the head of the pin, and in the nave or hub of the wheel there was always a 2in square gap on the outer edge to allow the pin to be pulled right out. The wheel was then slid off the axle and a good layer of thick cart grease, made from horse and other animal fats, was smeared onto the top part of the axle. The wheel would then be lifted back onto the axle in such a way as to leave as much grease as possible on top of the axle. Then the inside edge of the pin had to be greased and driven back into its hole in the axle. Before the jack was lowered the wheel was carefully spun to distribute the grease evenly. I remember the grease was always either thick black or a dirty yellow colour. Before the job was finished it was important that the lock was greased; this was the part on which the shafts turned, and if it wasn't well greased the horses would find it difficult to turn the cart.

'If he was travelling hilly country it was the waggoner's responsibility to take a skidpan with him: this was used to prevent the waggon from running away with a heavy load as it went downhill. For hilly country the waggoner would also need to be properly equipped for holding his waggon if the horses needed a "blow" – a breather – when going up the hill. Sometimes a wooden block would be used for this, but better still was a wooden roller about six inches in diameter; this would be hung behind the rear near wheel. Waggons were never fitted with brakes. At the bottom of a hill you had to be very careful when you

Steam-threshing at Romney Marsh between the wars

anaesthetic as you would have to now. There was blood absolutely everywhere and the cows were obviously in pain; we just sawed the horns off, and if you looked down the stump you could see into their skulls. It was terrible, but we knew no better then. If you left their horns to grow on they could do a lot of damage to each other and to you. We had one lovely old cow called Ghandi, and she was such a nice old thing we couldn't bring ourselves to cut her horns off; but being among a lot of cattle without horns she quickly realised that she could dominate them all, and became a terrible bully.

'I think the funniest thing I remember from my long farming years was the time I drove a flock of sheep into Stockton town centre. Driving sheep through big towns was an everyday occurrence at that time because there were no lorries and no other way to move them. Usually it went all right and the sheep stayed close together, but on this occasion for some unaccountable reason one of my sheep jumped straight through the plate-glass window of a shop. The sheep was all right, but the shopkeeper wasn't amused!'

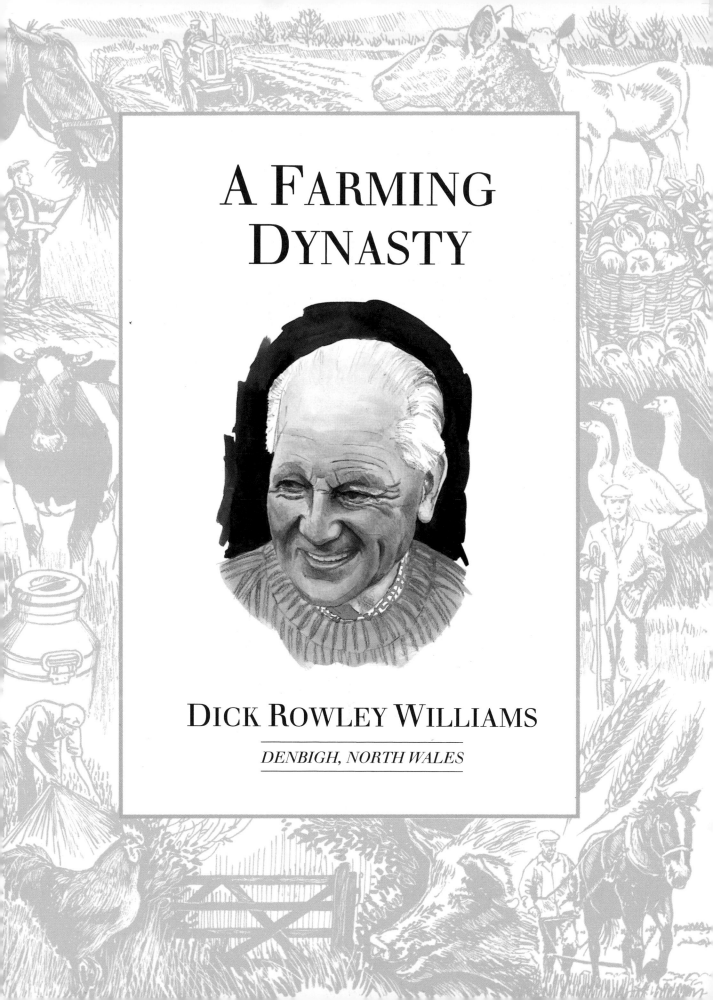

A FARMING
DYNASTY

DICK ROWLEY WILLIAMS

DENBIGH, NORTH WALES

Blundell Edward Rowley Williams, who is ninety-one, might easily be described as a gentleman farmer. But if this is taken to mean a farmer who simply gets others to do the work for him, then it will not do at all. For Mr Rowley Williams is a man who likes to get his hands dirty, and as well as indulging his lifelong enthusiasm for the gentlemanly pursuit of foxes, he has kept his remote Welsh farm going for seventy years through his own resources and hard work. Glyn Arthur is a lovely Regency house built by an ancestor, the family having owned the farm since the eighteenth century; it stands alone high on the Denbigh hills with glorious views of the town of Denbigh in the distance.

'Six generations of the family have now lived and worked here,' says Mr Rowley Williams, or Dick as he is known to friends and family. A quiet man who smiles readily and displays the formal good manners of a vanished era, he is proud of the family's long association with this part of Wales generally, and with Glyn Arthur in particular. 'My great-great-grandfather built the place using stone from a local quarry. We think work started on the house we see now in 1790, and it was certainly finished by 1800; but the old part of the house, to which my great-great-grandfather's house was "tacked on", as it were, has been here since about 1600. He could afford to build a new house simply because he had the good sense to marry an heiress. We haven't always been quite so sensible since!'

Although he is in his nineties, Dick still takes an active interest in the farm which is now run by his son Peter; farming seems to be bred in the family, although the different generations have approached it in markedly different ways. 'I suppose it was inevitable that I would be interested in farming, having been born here among farming people and where all the talk was of farming. But my own father was really what they call a gentleman farmer, in the sense that he had a private income and so didn't worry too much if the farm itself didn't make much money.'

'I was born in 1903, and my earliest memories are of riding various ponies. I loved horses and ponies – still do – and looking back now I seem to have spent my whole childhood on horseback. I rode from the time I was a very small boy; in fact it was unthinkable then for a boy, or indeed a girl, not to learn to ride – it was how we got about, and of course you couldn't hunt if you didn't ride, and all our friends and neighbours hunted. Hunting lay at the heart of all our social activities. I was perhaps three or four years old when I learned to ride, and I was still riding in my seventies. I was joint-master of the Flint and Denbigh hounds for more than fifty years, and my son is now joint-master; so hunting, like farming, is very much in the family. I was very keen on hunting from an early age, it was just so exciting, but of course when I was sent away to school at Shrewsbury I couldn't do much.'

After Shrewsbury, farming wasn't an automatic choice for a young man with good connections and a good

'My earliest memories are of riding various ponies...'

116

An early Fordson tractor in action at Glyn Arthur

education, and like many well-off country families, the Rowley Williamses decided that their son would benefit from spending some time abroad. 'When I left school I was sent to Rhodesia, largely I think because no one had the faintest idea what to do with me! I worked on a remote farm owned by a friend of the family, and all I remember is that after clearing the scrub using oxen, we grew tobacco and maize. I was also sent to France for a while to learn to speak the language. If you were brought up as a gentleman these were things you needed, and I suppose I could have gone into business and made a lot of money; but even then I dreaded the idea of working for someone else on a sort of five-days-a-week, nine-to-five basis.'

For Dick, the attractions of making money were as nothing compared to the attractions of hunting and shooting. 'Yes, I might have made more money if I'd done that sort of thing, but I realised pretty early on that I would be far happier farming, even if it meant making no money at all. The fact that I loved country life and everything it entailed also came into the decision, of course. If I were asked to sum up my life, I'd say that I didn't make much money but I enjoyed myself.

'I was also very keen on training and working sheepdogs. I never did this to win competitions, but simply because I enjoyed it – sheepdogs, and breeding and schooling horses. However, from an early age I worked on the farm, although we did employ farm-workers. I had to help with the horses, and with the sheep; in fact with just about everything, at one time or another.

'When I was a young man, shearing sheep was a far more exhausting and difficult business than it is now because it was all done with hand shears or clippers, like a big pair of iron scissors; a good man might shear forty sheep in a day, whereas nowadays a good

117

I remember once I was right at the top of a full haycart when the lead horse turned too quickly and I came off – I was lucky not to be injured. Farms are dangerous places, or they can be. On another occasion I got pushed right into a thick thorn hedge by a bull. I was in my suit as I'd just got back from town, when I found that our bull had got out of the field he shared with some heifers. I prodded him with a pickel, a small pitchfork, to encourage him to go back in through the gate, but he turned and chased me. I almost made it to the gate by the road, but not quite, and he hit me in the chest and ripped a great hole in my smart jacket. I was all right, but I was furious about my suit so I turned and shouted at him and waved my arms. I was so cross it worked and he turned and fled! But I must have looked very funny running across that field in my suit with my two dogs and a bull right behind me!

'In total I followed hounds from the age of six until the age of seventy-six, which may be some kind of record. I hunted with several packs and was chairman of the Flint and Denbigh hounds for many years. I had many falls, but few nasty ones. Once I went down with a horse that rolled on me, and had such a terrible bruise on my face that I couldn't shave for a week; it made my neck very bad too, so I went to an osteopath, but I think his treatment was worse than the injury – I thought he was going to wring my neck! Another time I was brought down by a pheasant, of all things, which flew through the horse's legs and made it stumble and down we went.

'Today we have just under one thousand sheep, and they graze our 380 acres as well as a sheep walk that we rent. We still have one farm-worker, but we couldn't possibly afford more and there'd be little for them to do because mechanisation and electricity and machines have made everything so much easier. We used to have a cook, two maids and a nanny, but those days are long gone. The nanny, who lived in, was paid £16 a year.

A land-girl at Glyn Arthur during the last war

Broadcasting seed on a steep Welsh hillside

'The only labour-saving device we had in my youth was a waterwheel. It was set up on the stream to drive our wood saw and to grind our corn. You just pulled up a sluice, the water came through, hit the wheel and you were in business.'

Like many country houses, Glyn Arthur had an inside loo by the turn of the century but it was reserved strictly for use by the women of the house; the men still had to go outside, and they continued to do so well into this century. The staff had another, entirely separate loo, which was also outside. Dick laughs indulgently now at how different things were in his youth; but he is proud that, however much things have changed, the presence of another generation of his family in the house is assured. He has four children: Peter, who now runs the farm; Richard, a civil engineer; Elizabeth, a solicitor; and Edmund who lives and works in London.

One characteristic of the Rowley Williamses which non-hunting people find curious is that, like most country people who love hunting they are very fond of the fox, and over the years have kept several as pets. 'We had one for a number of years when I was young, and if I shouted "Come on, Charlie!" he would rush over and jump into my arms. However, every fox will wander away eventually; I think the mating and travelling urge is just too strong and eventually they just have to go.

'Other foxes we kept used to wander around the house and sleep with the dogs. One used to play with the hounds – the fox would hide in the shrubbery in the garden while the hound puppies tried to find it. They'd draw for him in the undergrowth while he sat, with a rather superior look on his face, bang in the middle of the lawn!'

Towards the end of my day with Dick he confessed that, great though his love of farming is, he does occasionally regret that he did not devote more time to his other great love: art. From a dusty cupboard he revealed an ancient sketchbook filled with exquisite pictures of horses and ponies, sheep and other animals, landscapes and the hills of his beloved Wales. 'Yes, I studied art at an art school in the Home Counties for a while in the 1930s, because I had found I was quite good at it; but the farm was so busy that I did little over the years before Peter began to take over. But I have this book of drawings, and several of my pictures are framed on the walls here in the house, so there will at least be something of my artistic side when I'm gone.'

*Unloading and building
the stack*

GLEANINGS

Spanish Practices

THE successful attempts which have been made to improve the wools of England by an intermixture of the Spanish breed of sheep with South Downs and other flocks will not only increase the fineness but the softness of English clothing by increasing the amount of yolk contained in the fleece.

In the pure Spanish breed the supply of yolk is so plentiful that the use of an ointment for the wool may not be necessary. I would, however, recommend that immediately after shearing, the sheep should be rubbed on the back and sides with olive oil or a mix of olive oil, lard and wax, to preserve them from cold and wet.

Letters on the National Importance of Extending the Growth of Fine Clothing Wool, 1804

Farmhouse Fire

AND thus did I myself all alone quench a fire at a great farmhouse at Westoning in Bedfordshire, where coming that way accidentally and meeting a woman coming out of a yard and wringing her hands and crying I asked her the reason, but she gave no answer, but away she runs as fast as she could. I, fearing some such matter, run into the yard, but finding the door locked and hearing withall a fluttering of fire, I took up an hog's trough which lay there and ran against the door and broke it open and went in.

Where I found a great many turves had fired all the timber of the chimney. I, having been at the fuller's earth pits, not far from Oburn, to survey them, threw ashes into the chimney and finding a pail, I ran and fetched turf ashes and water together and quenched all quite in a quarter of an hour. All this while not one body came. So I was going hence and as I was going out at the gate there came near half a score, which she had brought out of the field from haying.

George Atwell, *The Faithfull Surveyour*, 1663

Moistening the Land

YET this I have seen in one of those dry years in a meadow near Hartford that one man, having a piece of land encompassed with the river, flowing it made five pound of an acre of his first crop where his neighbour made scarce twenty shillings an acre of the ground adjoining; yet this is not comparable to land floods, for these partaking of a muddy and slimy substance being brought into meadows and pastures in the spring, either by drains, darks, turning of town ditches, sewers, highways, streets, filths, do both moisten and fat them, whereas the river water fats nothing so much.

George Atwell, *The Faithfull Surveyour*, 1663

Curse of Enclosure

THESE new enclosures and houses arise out of the beggaring of the parts of the country distant from the vortex of the funds. The farmhouses have long been growing fewer and fewer; the labourers' houses fewer and fewer, and it is manifest to every man who has eyes to see with, that the villages are regularly wasting away.

This is the case all over the parts of the kingdom where the tax eaters do not haunt. In all of the really agricultural villages and parts of the kingdom, there is a shocking decay; a great dilapidation and constant pulling down or falling down of houses. The farmhouses are not so many as they were forty years ago by three-fourths. That is to say the infernal system of Pitt and his followers has annihilated three parts out of four of the farmhouses. The labourers' houses disappear also. And all the useful people become less numerous.

William Cobbett, *Rural Rides*, 1830

Farming by Experiment

BUT the world is now grown so incredulous that they cannot believe that a man will become bald by being shaved at the wrong time of the moon, without more experience has been made of it for these 1,700 years past. If all these phantasies delivered down to us from the ancients be looked on as mere fables why should we acquiesce in following a pretended maxim which, though it has deceived some part of the world a great while, doth, when brought to the test of experiment prove fallacious. The experience of 1,700 years no more proves a practice to be right than the long experience of cattel drawing by their tails proved that practice right, before drawing by traces was by experiment proved to be better; for nothing can be depended on as experience, which has not been tried by experiment.

Jethro Tull, *Horse-hoeing Husbandry*, 1829

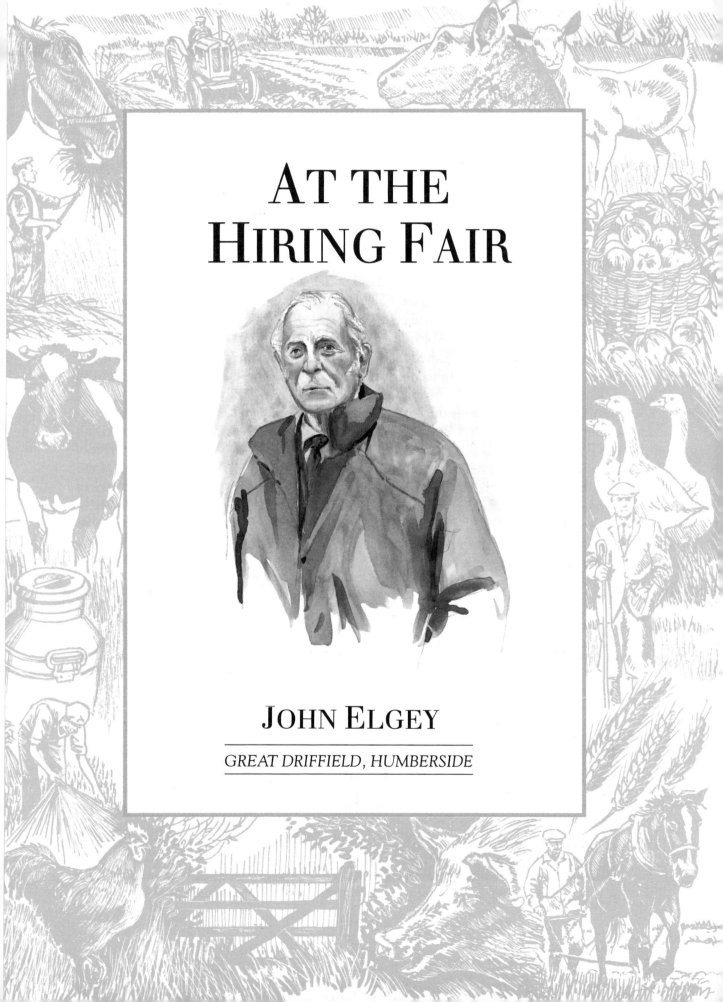

AT THE
HIRING FAIR

JOHN ELGEY

GREAT DRIFFIELD, HUMBERSIDE

'The horsemen started at six in the morning and finished at six at night.'

'The workmen would always ask "Is it a good meat house?": meaning, would they get plenty to eat. Some would want to know how much salmon they would have to eat, which was a serious question because farms on estates where there were salmon rivers were often fed on fish from the river every day for weeks through the summer, and they didn't like it. Or up towards Whitby they'd worry that the farmer would give them sea fish every day because it was cheaper than meat.'

John explained that men at the hiring fair were almost always taken on for the year; it meant that if they left after six months they weren't paid a penny. They received their full wages at the end of the year, which may seem hard by today's standards, but, again, it was a system handed down from time immemorial. 'That was the way it had been done for longer than anyone could remember, and in those days people didn't dare to deviate from the way things were supposed to be done.'

However, what may sound like a kind of slavery in theory often worked rather well in practice, since the farm-worker would have little time for leisure, and he could be sure of a roof over his head as well as board and lodging for the whole period of his year-long contract with the farmer. 'Some men were quite happy where they worked; our foreman and his wife, for example, stayed with us for thirty-seven years and the wife used to cook for the men. All twelve used to sleep in one big bedroom which we called the dormitory, with two men to a bed; the foreman's wife made the beds every day. It all seems like another world now, but that's the way it was.'

The late summer rain began to beat down on us as evening came on, so John took me into the house and showed me a couple of items from his museum of farm equipment: a tiny child's hayfork, and a wide, beautifully polished grain shovel especially made to avoid bruising the corn. A few well-made pieces of heavy oak furniture around the sitting-room have been handed down through succeeding generations of his family. John explained how the farming year was organised when he was a young man in the 1920s:

'It was pretty straightforward. You tried to get all your wheat sown by Martinmas, that is, by November, and then you carried on ploughing through the winter so there was land ready to be sown with barley and oats in the spring. The weather had to be pretty atrocious for you not to get out in the fields because the work had to be done in time; you just got wet, but with a thick wool coat and a sack over you, you didn't get too cold, and anyway you were working too hard to get cold!

'Our plough teams consisted of two horses and a plough with a single furrow eight or nine inches wide. The ploughman always had a boy with him, and the head ploughman always started up the field with the others setting off behind him and to the side following his line. Boys following learned how to plough simply by watching the ploughman. A boy might start at twelve years old and take a plough at thirteen or perhaps fourteen, but by then if he was destined to be a ploughman he would already have learned a lot during his holidays from school and in his spare time. Though the ploughman's life was hard, a ploughman's son wouldn't be wanting to stay at school rather than going on the land: he'd be itching to follow his father. I suppose like all children it was simply a question of wanting to be grown up.

'It's fairly simple to plough across the field, but on the headland the plough could easily tip over because you didn't have an existing furrow to keep the thing even, and of course it was very tiring to get it good and straight and even unless you really knew what you were doing. That's where the real skill came in. Up on the headland you let it run on the heel of the plough and on the long-shanked wheel. After your first mark across the field you came back on yourself and it was easier, but drawing that first furrow was a real skill. We called it a rig, that is, the furrows and the high ground on the land. These days the reversible plough doesn't leave ridges and furrows as the old ploughs used to, and of course it's much quicker. With horses, the speed depended a lot on how fit the horses were and on the skill of the ploughman. Of course if the ploughman was particularly good and keen at his work, things went very well.'

Thistles

someone's garden as you drove them along the road it was the householder's fault if his roses were eaten. These days if your cattle eat someone's roses it's your fault. Cattle were walked regularly from Scotland to Smithfield Market in London, and townspeople were used to seeing animals about the town.

'I remember Dad buying cattle in York market, which was along the old wall of the city; the cattle would be milling around in the road and Dad would bargain with the owner. I remember once he bought some Irish store bullocks which had been driven all the way from Liverpool across to York on the roads. And after we bought them they were walked to the farm along the roads.

'Though farm work was hard in the 1930s no one ever worked on Sundays unless it was very urgent indeed. Now, because so few people work on the farms you have to work on Sundays pretty regularly. But the work isn't as hard physically now – in the 1930s you were following a plough or tossing hay all day with a fork so you had to have a day off just to recover, quite apart from any religious commitment.

'A lot of workers were itinerant: every year at harvest-time in August and September bands of men would come and were contracted for a month's work. Often they would have walked here from the Yorkshire Dales where the haymaking was a little earlier. Many men came to the same farms year after year, and their sons followed them; after leaving us they would go down to Lincolnshire for the potato-picking, and that way they gradually walked round the country picking up the seasonal jobs, as they picked them up year after year.

'These days a lot of our hedges are gone; you need them if you have sheep and so on, but for the big machines we use now they are a bit of a nuisance. We don't lose land here when the wind blows so we don't need hedges to prevent erosion as they do on some farms.'

The Elgeys have been farming since the early 1700s. From his own research John has discovered that the family was first recorded at a 400-acre farm on the Yorkshire Wolds, about eight miles from Bainton, and he believes they would have taken that first farm soon after the great enclosures of the late eighteenth century. 'I know it was land that had never been farmed before.' he says. 'It was wasteland when they started, we know that. They owned that farm, but it was bought for what was called "three lives", in other words for three generations only; then it went back to the original owner. This was true of many farms in those days. We were in an odd situation here, too, because although we rented this farm, Dad owned another one nearby that someone else worked. He sold that farm during World War II, however, which was probably a mistake.

'My father died just after the last war and I ran the farm until a few years ago when my nephew took over. Although I have no children of my own, I like to think it will be carried on by a member of the family when I'm gone.'

BUTTON HOOKS AND BRITCHES

AUBREY CHARMAN

HORSHAM, SUSSEX

found it was alive and well and back in the pig house! All we could think was that the heat from the manure had driven the pneumonia out of it and revived it!'

Many of the everyday items of food that we now take for granted were difficult, if not impossible, to obtain earlier this century. Other items such as fish were a rare treat for inland families like the Charmans. 'Over the years from 1920 until about 1936 we children would listen out for the sound of a bell ringing on the main Worthing Road. Immediately we heard it, my mother would give me a shilling and tell me to run up to the road because it was the mackerel seller, a man with a big horse-drawn cart piled high with thousands of mostly mackerel and herrings. He would have started early that morning on the south coast, and gradually worked his way towards London selling his fish at every village along the way. We usually got thirty herrings for a shilling, and sometimes more if there were only a few left, because by the time he reached us, the fish man would usually have had enough and would not be wanting to go further. If he did, he had to go up Picks Hill at Horsham which was very steep; in fact it was much steeper than it is today, and to get up it you had to hire two extra horses at the foot of the hill at the toll gate; they were kept there specifically for this purpose. You can still see how steep the hill originally was if you look at the two sides of the cutting the council made to reduce its steepness.

'Between 1915 and about 1935 there was another oddity on the road, one which almost everyone forgets these days: the steam engine. The steamers, as they were known, needed a lot of water so village ponds near the road were kept as free as possible of rubbish so they could fill up as they went along.'

Aubrey would be the first to agree that in the old days the countryside produced many eccentrics. They were usually tolerated, however quirky their behaviour might become, but it is wrong to think that they were always amusing; some were probably simply reclusive. Aubrey remembers one noted Southwater character whose reputation as an eccentric was based largely on the fact that he was extremely antisocial:

'Bernard Green died in 1979. He would have been about seventy-five, I think, but I remembered him from when he was twenty and he came to work for my father. He was a most conscientious worker, but nothing would induce him to get to work before nine o'clock and as that upset all the other farm-workers who started at seven, we had to get rid of him. When he left he rented about twenty acres of land and reared stock. But he would help any farmer at harvest-time. He was often seen digging potatoes late at night by the light of a lamp, but you'd never see him doing it during daylight. He never mixed with the villagers, and lived in some poverty in a cottage in New Road. He was often seen returning from his cattle well after midnight. When finally he was found dead he was in his bed with his overcoat and boots on, and all around him were scattered cattle sales cheques going back years which he'd never bothered to pay into the bank. Although he lived in Southwater for more than sixty years I don't suppose he was known to more then twenty people, and he had no friends.

'Animals can be eccentric, too; each one has its own character, and occasionally you'll get one that is remarkable in some way – like our mare Dolly. She was used as a trace horse: when we were carting mangolds or whatever from a very wet field, the waggon would sink into the mud; so using a special chain harness we would add Dolly to the horse already harnessed to the waggon. When the load had been pulled across the field to the hard road, the man in charge would unhitch Dolly, hang the chains over her back and turn her round. She'd then set off on her own across the field precisely to the front of the next loaded cart, and she would do this all by herself twenty times a day. She was a lovely horse with a marvellous nature, and she worked for us for twenty-three years before we pensioned her off.

'Another horse we had wasn't so amenable. She used to be in a terrible hurry to get out of her harness and start feeding when we tried to unhitch her in the evenings; she got so bad that she'd sometimes break out of the harness, and we knew that eventually someone would get hurt. We cured her by putting a coat over her head before unhitching her and leading her to within a couple of feet of the stable wall. Of course she bolted as usual, but this time she hit the wall and knocked herself out – but she never rushed again.

'Horses could be marvellous. Every morning our seven would be tied together, and entirely on their own they would leave the stable in line and walk eighty yards down to the pond to drink before returning to the stable for breakfast. They always did the whole thing on their own, at the same pace and in the same time. It was a marvel to see.

'Horsham market was started in 1852; it has long gone, but we used to go by horse, or on foot driving the sale animals, and it was a fair sight to see. There would be sheep, cattle, chickens and rabbits everywhere, and you would always see a number of Jews, who came down from London to buy poultry and rabbits.

'For as long as anyone could remember, and certainly until the end of World War II when new hygiene regulations made it impossible, most villagers kept a pig or two in a sty built at the bottom of the garden. They bought the smaller piglets, known as "dolly" pigs or "runts", from a farmer's litter, and reared them on boiled scraps, milk, curds, and buttermilk. In the autumn they would go "gleaning" which was a family affair, to collect corn-heads spilled at harvesting. I've known a family collect several bushels of corn-heads which were fed to the pigs for several weeks. When half-grown, the pigs were sent to the butcher for killing, and he would buy half, while the other half was taken back by the cottager to be smoked in the chimney for use during the winter. The same could be done today, except that modern law does not permit the smell of a pig in the garden in housing estates. The great thing about keeping a pig was that it didn't need much space and you could feed it on anything; we feed ours on dead chickens and dead rabbits with the feathers and fur on, bad cabbage and apples, damp corn going mouldy and absolutely any waste vegetables from the kitchen. They thrived on everything. I even remember one farmer whose land was infested with rabbits: every evening he took the Land Rover and his gun, and shot up to thirty rabbits which he then fed to his pigs, as meal at that time was very dear. For two months those pigs lived on unskinned, uncooked rabbits and what is more, looked very well on it. Pigs will eat almost anything, even bones, and can successfully convert any waste foods.

'Nowadays most farmers specialise in one or two products in a big way, where seventy years ago they would have kept a few of all types of livestock, including geese, turkeys and farmyard fowls. My grandfather and his father kept large black lop-eared pigs which were known as Sussex pigs. They were easy to control because their ears covered their eyes, which meant that if they tried to run off they would bang into things because they couldn't see! Our breeding sows were driven out every day to graze grass, and in the autumn walked to the woods to feed on acorns. As boys, my father and his brother used to take the pigs out to certain fields before they went to school each day, and they would fetch them back in the evening, after school.

'On one occasion, three of our sows were due to farrow at the same time, so one shed was filled with straw. The sows were brought in that night and they made a cosy hole in the straw. The next day they had all farrowed, so they were trough fed, near their young. Three days later the little pigs had all appeared and were running about, and there was a record number: fifty-one, seventeen per sow. The sows were sisters and happily suckled each other's piglets, so no one really knew the correct mothers or how many each mother had had. My father assured me these facts were true, so pigs have not improved in performance today since the average for the best herds is now ten and a half piglets reared. Black pigs have all but disappeared because modern housewives don't like the black pigment caused by the skin; also the Middle White, snub-nosed pigs which were very popular thirty years ago as they were good doers and very fat are now almost extinct, as people have gone off fat.'

Aubrey's memories of animal husbandry,

Aubrey's father, Edgar, in about 1914

160

and of the everyday life of farm and village early this century are remarkably precise, and he is also one of the few still alive who can remember seeing men wearing that most English of farm-workers' garments, the smock: 'For more than two hundred years all agricultural workers in Sussex and many other areas wore a smock – it was actually a kind of overcoat. It went out of use just after the Great War in this area, but I can remember the men wearing them. The Sussex smock was a long bell-shaped garment which had no buttons but had to be slipped over your head. They were rather heavy, especially when dressed with tallow – the fat from which candles were made – to make them waterproof. Nevertheless, if you were ploughing all day in the rain this waterproofing was a great asset. Most workers and farmers kept a second, clean white smock for attending church.'

Like many farmers and farm-workers who grew up during the early years of this century, Aubrey built up an immunity to TB, the disease which was once endemic in British cattle; in fact, either you became immune or you died.

'Our cows were first tested in the spring of 1920, and twenty-seven out of thirty were found to have TB; under the law, these had to be slaughtered. To my father and I this was a great disappointment as they *looked* perfectly healthy. It wasn't a total disaster, however, because we were given money in compensation for our loss. With this in his pocket, my father went to the north of England and bought replacement cows which had passed all the TB tests.

'Twelve months later, after the cows had been housed all winter, a second test was carried out for TB, and imagine our disappointment when twenty-five out of thirty cows failed! My father promptly called in the vet, who phoned the head of the ministry's veterinary department; we received a visit from the ministry, and were told that we had to build an outside yard so that the air could blow through night and day. We could use the old enclosed cowshed for milking only; but should turn the cows out again into the outside yard as soon as fresh straw had been spread.

'What had been happening was this: a cow with what might have been dormant TB germs breathed against the wall of the cowshed, and in the hot, enclosed atmosphere the next cow caught the germs. She then passed it on to the next cow, and so on until virtually every cow was infected. Remember, the cows spent five months in this cowhouse, and evidently the temperature was so hot the TB spread very rapidly. On this clay soil all our cows must be housed for the five long winter months even today, but they are kept in open yards and we haven't had a case of TB in any animal for thirty years.

'To encourage farmers, in 1920 the Government paid an extra 4d per gallon on milk proved free of TB. But as a child I had a glass of milk for supper every night, and I must have drunk many a gallon of tubercular milk. Because nature builds an immunity to most diseases in children, I have remained very healthy, although I must admit I've never been tested for TB. I think cattle are now more healthy than most humans because they get tested for things so often. It is still every two years for TB!'

Amongst the most interesting medieval survivals that Aubrey remembers were the faggots used to light ovens and heat coppers. Faggots were bundles of wood about six feet long, tied in the centre, and about nine inches in diameter. For centuries in Sussex and elsewhere all bread was baked in ovens that had first been heated with faggots. Two or three were set alight in the oven, which was usually a great brick-built thing, or a smaller

'We used to go by horse, or on foot driving the sale animals…'

Georeorge Greenheld spent most of his working life among the sheep and horses of the Yorkshire Wolds. Now seventy-one, he retired officially many years ago; but the farmers in his part of Yorkshire still know that if they're having problems at lambing time, George is far more likely to be able to help than the local vet. For George is one of the old school, a man whose knowledge is based not on books and theory, but on a lifetime spent among the animals he tended. He was born in Edstone near Kirby Moorside in 1923. His younger days were hard by any standards, and although he will argue that on the whole he has had a rich, fulfilling life, he still smiles and shakes his head in good-humoured astonishment at the changes he has witnessed in his lifetime:

'I don't think another generation will ever live through such changes again. When I was a lad you never saw a car, or if you did if was a real event. Everything was moved about on waggons, and a young lad knew he would do more or less as his father and grandfather had done as soon as he was old enough.' For generations the Greenhelds earned their living on the land or in occupations intimately connected with farm work and agriculture. George's grandfather, for example, was a waggon driver for a big grain mill at Pickering; he could neither read nor write, but worked diligently for many years carting grain from Pickering to Scarborough along the slow roads – and they were slow, as George explains:

'Shires and work horses never trotted, let alone cantered; always a steady walk, and the pace of life was dictated by the horse. No one in those days moved faster than a horse could move.'

George's father farmed at Kirbymoorside and although many of George's memories of childhood are happy ones, his early years were marked by a series of disasters: 'My father was killed by a farm horse when I was just twelve years old. Mother left the farm after that and we went to live in a cottage in Pickering. But we were there only about a year when Mother died, too, and I was put out to work for some relatives. I don't want to go into that too much because they made my life hell – working there was one of the worst experiences of my life. They paid me £25 a year and tried to work me to death; it got so bad that eventually I ran away. They treated me like a slave. I was up at 5.30 every morning seven days a week, and had to work right through till six at night whatever the weather.'

What must have made the back-breaking, thankless tasks of those years much worse was the fact that George had been struck down by polio at about the time his father was killed. His brother fell victim to the disease at the same time and died, but George survived – just. He was helped by an uncle.

'The doctor in the hospital to which I was sent said that I would never be able to walk again – but then I didn't like that doctor much; I think he liked having us there so he could observe and experiment on us, and I don't think he thought of us as human beings. Anyway, he gave me no encouragement at all

A ploughman tests the soil

'So I rode over to them... on my bike'

as I lay there unable to walk. An old uncle of mine helped me in the end – he worked as a gamekeeper and lived in an old cottage well off the road, and he agreed to have me when I came out of hospital. I couldn't walk then, so he met me where the bus put me down and carried me more than a mile on his back to his cottage. In the days that followed he made me two little walking sticks and told me I could certainly walk again if I just kept at it. And do you know, soon after that I was able to drop one stick and then the other. It was hard though, very hard. But once I was rid of the second stick I never looked back, and the fact that I have always walked with a bit of a limp has made not the slightest difference to my life. I've always done what I've wanted to do.'

Being his own man and able to do just as he pleases has clearly always been important to George – 'I could always ride a horse as well as any man' he says proudly – which is why he eventually chose to flee from the farm where he had started work. 'They would have worked me to death otherwise, I think. I had to milk twelve cows and get the churns filled at the side of the road every day by eight o'clock, then clean out the byres and feed the cattle; then I had to go round the sheep, pull turnips and cart fodder. The food was very poor, too. I put up with it for two years, and then a friend who worked on a big farm owned by the Hon George Vestey told me they needed a cattleman. So I rode over to them – eight miles on my bike – and the boss agreed to see me; as it was Martinmas week I was able to take the job they offered straightaway. The farmworker's term of employment ran from one Martinmas to the next in those days. My old boss told me he wouldn't let me go, so I packed my tin – all farm lads and labourers had tin trunks for their things in those days – and upped and left. I just ran for it.'

The new farm was a big improvement, and George was paid the splendid sum of thirty shillings a fortnight, plus overtime. After two bitter years as a slave to people who were supposed to be his family, it was a real relief. 'Oh, I was in clover there,' he says, with a beaming happy smile. 'Six men lived in and we all got along. They were older than me, but good honest men and so helpful. I had a bit more free time, too, so sometimes we used to go to the pictures at Pocklington on our bikes and then have fish and chips and a bottle of Vimto afterwards – and all for 1s 6d! We also played dominoes and cards in the evenings, but generally went to bed early; you had to, because you had to be up early again next day. We would visit the lads on other farms round about, too, and compare our masters and our situations. I spent three years at this farm. However, it was only when I

'You were out in the air, the gulls wheeling overhead...'

left and moved to a farm near Scarborough that I came to work among horses. They'd been around before, of course, but then I was a cattleman and hadn't worked much with them.'

In fact George worked full time with horses at his next farm, Scalby Lodge; he had taken work there in order to be closer to his sister who had moved to Scarborough. The horses were his direct responsibility: 'I loved working with the horses. We'd get up at 5.30, groom them, feed them, and then go in for our own breakfast at 6.45. At 7.30 we'd get them harnessed and set off for the fields. Ploughmen often rode to the fields, though never sitting astride, always sideways on the horse. That slow morning ride was worth a lot to me, the gentle movement of the massive horse and the view from that height, sitting up on his back, over the hedges and across the fields. We ploughed with a single-furrow plough, and with the horses side by side, one in the furrow and one on the land – that is, on the bit yet to be ploughed.'

George insists that ploughing was a serious, skilled business, far more so than it would be with a modern tractor, because apart from the difficulties of controlling the horses, the old ridge-and-furrow technique involved cutting much deeper into the land than the more modern method. But although the work was hard, it had its compensations: 'Although you walked many miles in a day's ploughing it was lovely work, even if the weather was bad. You were out in the air, the gulls wheeling overhead, the wind clearing out the cobwebs. Ploughing was certainly more difficult than it is today, but you knew that if you were working with good horses they would make up for any of your shortcomings. It was a sort of team effort and you were aware of it. You see how much team effort you can get out of a tractor!'

And the comradeship of working with the horses was matched, it seems, by the comradeship of working with other skilled men; there was a sense of belonging among farm-workers generally, and in particular among the workers on any one farm – they would go around together, drinking and playing as a distinct group during the few hours of freedom they had each week. However, it wasn't all sweetness and light: some farmers and their foremen would quickly earn themselves a reputation as unreasonable or oppressive, and workers would go to them only as a last resort. Nevertheless, according to George such men were in a minority, and generally speaking if you pulled your weight you were among friends:

'Other workers would try to help you if they could, and they'd always be good with a new lad who'd perhaps never ploughed before because a lad's first day at the plough could be awful for him even if it was a bit of fun for the rest of us – he'd be bound to get in a mess a few times. The solution on most farms was to give a new lad a pair of experienced horses to see him right, and he would never be expected to draw the first furrow across the field; that was always done by an experienced man, because the line set would be the line all the subsequent furrows followed – if the first was wrong, they'd all be wrong, and all the other ploughmen round about would soon know if so-and-so had made a bad job of a field. The art of the thing was to plough straight, and if you could do that you were doing well.'

Virtual self-sufficiency was an important aspect of life on a farm early this century; thus the food the workers ate was produced on the farm, and farms would breed, train and work their own horses. 'All the farms on which I worked bred their own horses for farm work, though one or two would also breed them to be sold. One farm I worked on sold them to the brewers – all the brewers round about had teams of horses to pull the drays. They still keep horses to this day, but only for special occasions. And what few people know is that each brewer would only take horses of a particular colour, so Tetley would only ever have grey horses, for example, while Youngs insisted on black.'

In some parts of the country the practice was for farm horses to work right through the day without returning to their stables at midday. However, in George's part of Yorkshire the horses were always taken back to the stable at noon and fed before the men went in for the main meal of the day. 'We always fed the horses at midday like this and we got their feed ready for the night. After we'd finished our dinner, about one o'clock, we'd go out again and work through till about 7pm.'

Although the men had heard about the new tractors that were beginning to show up here and there in the 1930s, few had seen one, except perhaps as an exhibit at a show, and it was hard to imagine that tractors would ever really change the nature of land work for ever. 'There wasn't a single tractor round here,' says George, 'not one, they were unheard of, so far as I know. But we were too busy getting through the long days to worry much about them, or to imagine that they would ever make life easier for us.'

George and his plough team in 1944

The boys ran with Scrooey-Looey down to the river, over the bridge on to the water-meadow and jumped into a boat. Julius took one oar, Alexander the other and began to row up river. Benjamin and the rabbit sat in the prow and quickly fell asleep.

They rowed upstream until they reached a cave.

"It looks very dark," said Julius.

"I don't like it," cried Alexander.

"Let's go back," added Benjamin, who had awoken with a start.

Julius and Alexander tried to turn the boat, to row back to the water-meadow, but it would not turn: it headed upstream by itself.

The boys and the rabbit huddled together in the bottom of the boat as it travelled upstream through the cave, the light of the entrance becoming smaller and smaller as the boat travelled faster and faster. It stopped at a landing jetty in a vast cavern, stone steps rising up towards a faint green light. They got out of the boat and full of fear walked towards the steps.

A figure emerged from the sickly light. "Welcome! Welcome!" cried the witch Griselda. "I am very pleased to see you."

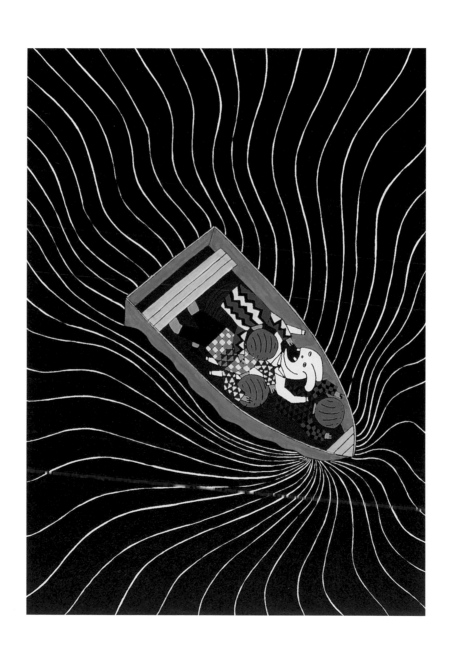

Drawn by the power of Griselda's magic, the boys and Scrooey-Looey climbed the steps, left the dark cavern and entered the family vault, deep below the ruined tower. Griselda's dead ancestors stood in glass tanks, their flesh preserved in special fluid. Their evil spirit bubbled up through tubes stuck in their heads and was collected in dark bottles, a lovely drink (or so Griselda thought).

"Let me introduce you to Baron Rufus de Grunch, the founder of the family," said Griselda pointing to a bearded man standing in a glass tank, axe and spear in hand. "He was very fond of boys."

"She means he ate them," whispered Scrooey-Looey, as the boys and rabbit hurried out of the family vault, through the dungeon, out of the hall, into the glade deep within the forest.

"Guards, come here!" bellowed Griselda. The three dwarves came running. "Put them in the cages, fatten them up, cook them for supper." Griselda went back into the tower leaving the dwarves to get to work.

The boys fought hard. By the time the dwarves, Julioso, Aliano and Benjio, got the boys in the cages and fed them with the fattening mixture they were tired out. Griselda had left her magic staff beside the magic cauldron.

"Roasting, stewing and toasting boys is hard work. Let's cook them by magic," suggested Julioso, who was dim and did not know you cannot cook boys by magic: there is too much fun and wildness in them.

The dwarves were puzzled: in none of Griselda's books could they find a spell for cooking boys. In the end they said the spell for cooking unicorns (changing the word 'unicorn' to 'boys and rabbit'). What happened next was surprising. All the snakes and creepy spiders in the glade got up and started ballroom dancing and the boys and Scrooey-Looey disappeared

II

The boys and the rabbit were in what looked like a lost luggage office, except that instead of umbrellas there were top hats, silk handkerchiefs, and magic wands.

Goblins hurried in, saw Scrooey-Looey and groaned: "Not another rabbit. Magicians are always losing rabbits." They seized Scrooey-Looey by the arms and threw him out the door.

The boys were angry. "You can't do that." "That's Scrooey-Looey." "He's our friend."

The goblins ignored them. "Now what have we here?" They looked carefully at the brothers and consulted a book. "Boys. It says here that magicians are forbidden to make boys disappear. If these three boys are part of an illegal act perhaps the magician will not dare to claim them. In three months we can sell them in the market. Lock them up."

The goblins seized the boys and locked them in the strongroom, where they found a lady sawn in two, waiting patiently, her top half knitting, her bottom half practising a tap dance. "Where is Jerry?" she sighed. "I left the supper in the oven. If he doesn't hurry, it will be burnt." She continued knitting and dancing, talking all the time:

"Who is Jerry? My husband. A magician. The most useless magician in the world. I end up here once or twice a week. Where are we? The Lost Magic Office. When a spell goes wrong you end up here. Sensible, really. You can't go hunting through the universe for things which have been magicked by mistake. So everything travels here. The magician comes, pays a small fine, and collects his lost property or assistant."

"What happens if he does not come?"

"Oh, after three months if you have not been collected, they sell you in the market."

She continued talking. "Only the magician who magicked you here can get you out. What was her name? Griselda! Not a nice name. Not nice at all. Would not go down well with our audience. Jerry is the Great Fernando. I'm his assistant Esdermelda. Sounds better than Jerry and Sylvie. Perhaps this Griselda will come and get you out."

"We do hope not," said the boys. "We would prefer to be sold in the market."

The door opened and a little man in a top hat scurried in. "My dear, I am so sorry. Such a silly mistake."

"Never mind. Just put me together before the supper's burnt."

The little man raised a magic wand and the two parts of Sylvie joined together. "Thank goodness for that," said Sylvie. "I never feel quite right when I am sawn in two."

The boys were miserable: "Either we are collected by Griselda or sold in the market." "A very gloomy outlook." "Not good at all."

"Where is Scrooey-Looey?" asked Benjamin. "Perhaps he can get us out."

The boys looked out of the window (which had heavy bars). "There he is." "Scrooey-Looey!" the boys all shouted.

Scrooey-Looey turned, waved, squeaked excitedly, "They've just opened a new lettuce bar," and ran off.

Time passed slowly. Once or twice a week Sylvie appeared, sometimes whole, sometimes in two parts. She cheered them up. "Hello boys. Still here. Where is that rabbit friend of yours? Still at the lettuce bar? What a shame."

One day the boys heard the sound of shouting from the office outside the strongroom: Griselda was trying to claim them.

"Madam," said a goblin politely, "that would be against the rules. They were magicked here by three dwarves. Only the dwarves can claim them. Madam, you are not a dwarf."

"Of course I am not a dwarf," shrieked Griselda. "The dwarves belong to me. They are my property."

"That does not change Rule 33(2)(b)," said the goblin. "Only the person who magicked the property can reclaim it."

Griselda screamed and stamped her feet. "Very well, I shall return tomorrow with the dwarves but the boys must not escape. If I pay you £50 will you chain them to the wall?" The goblin agreed.

The boys had a dreadful night chained to the wall but just as it was getting light Scrooey-Looey awoke them, took a piece of metal out of his pocket and quickly picked the locks. The boys and rabbit hurried outside. An alarm went off. "Lost property escaping!" screeched the goblins, grabbing their spears. Griselda arrived with her guards, sounded her hunting horn, and bellowed "Tally ho! Off we go! Let's get them."

The goblins, Griselda and the dwarves chased them past the lettuce bar, through a wood, across a rocky hillside. They were only just behind them when the boys and rabbit saw a cave and hurried inside. There was a hiss and the entrance to the cave snapped shut. "Oh dear! I think we have been eaten," cried the boys.

When the goblins, dwarves and Griselda saw the snake, one hundred foot long, six foot high and wide, they shook with horror. Its tongue shot out, knocked the magic staff out of Griselda's hand and threw it far away: goblins, dwarves and Griselda screamed and fled.

III

"What do we do now?" asked the boys. "It's not very nice being stuck inside a snake."

Scrooey-Looey took the piece of metal out of his pocket and tickled the inside of the snake. The snake shook, wriggled, opened its mouth, hissed, "Stop it! Stop it!" then burped and sent boys and rabbit flying through the air into a nearby forest.

It was dark and creepy there. Suddenly Alexander yelped: "Julius did you pinch me?"

"No, I did not."

"You've done it again!"

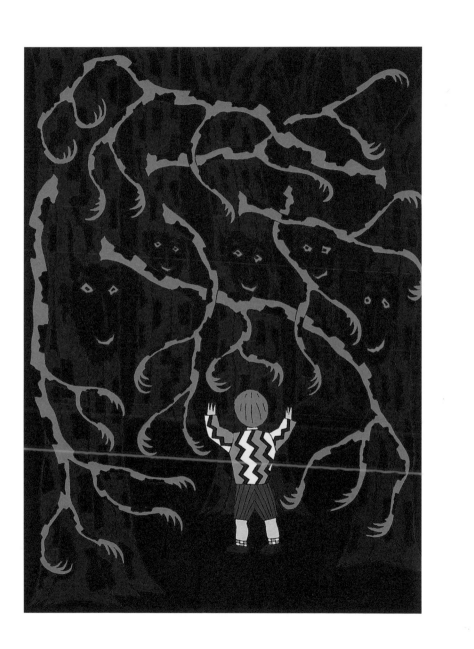

There was an evil chuckle. "It was the branches of that tree," cried Benjamin. The tree trunk had green eyes and a leering mouth. It chuckled again as it stretched out a twiggy branch and pinched Alexander hard.

"It's creeping nearer," screamed Benjamin in horror.

"Oh help!" cried Scrooey-Looey, shaking like a jelly.

All around the boys and rabbit were trees with evil eyes and leering mouths. They were slowly edging closer, bending down their twiggy branches and twiggy fingers to pinch the boys and rabbit hard. "Run, run, run!" cried Julius, taking Benjamin and Scrooey-Looey by the hand.

They ran and ran when, from between the trees, there appeared Globerous Ghosts. Globerous Ghosts are the fattest, ooziest ghosts that have ever lived. A single touch from their arms will turn a boy (or rabbit) into a ghostly glob.

In front of the boys and rabbit stretched a deep, black pond. Behind them, floating ever nearer, came the Globerous Ghosts with outstretched arms.

"We are trapped!" screamed Alexander.

The boys and the rabbit huddled together, quaking with fear. The Globerous Ghosts had nearly got them when from the pond there came a glug, glug, glug. It was the ducky rocky.

The ducky rocky's ancestors had grown a shell of rock as protection from hunters' guns but his shell had become so heavy that the ducky rocky could not fly or float. He lived upon the bottom of the pond coming up once or twice a day for air. To swim to the surface was terribly hard work.

With great splashing the ducky rocky emerged, gasped for air and cried, "Stick out your tongues," then sank to the bottom of the pond.

The boys stuck out their tongues.

The one thing Globerous Ghosts cannot stand is boys who stick their tongues out. As soon as they saw the boys sticking out their tongues the Globerous Ghosts exploded into a thousand ghostly globs which splattered all around the forest.

"That was a lucky escape," gasped the boys, putting in their tongues.

The boys and rabbit had hardly stopped shaking when from between the trees there appeared Mystic Mummies. Mystic Mummies are the most evil mummies that have ever lived. A single touch from their arms will turn a boy (or rabbit) into a pile of dust.

The boys and rabbit huddled together, quaking with fear. The Mystic Mummies had nearly got them when from the pond there came a glug, glug, glug.

"Come on, ducky rocky. Come on! Come on! Tell us what to do," cried the boys, as the Mystic Mummies stretched out their arms to turn them into dust.

The ducky rocky was swimming as hard as he could. He reached the surface, gasped for air, cried, "Pick your noses," then sank to the bottom of the pond.

The boys picked their noses. The one thing Mystic Mummies cannot stand is boys who pick their noses. As soon as they saw the boys picking their noses they screamed, "Germs! Germs!" Their bandages unravelled and blew away in the wind; their innards turned to dust.

"Lucky escape," murmured the boys, taking their fingers out of their noses.

The boys and rabbit had not stopped shaking when from between the trees there appeared Venomous Vampires, dressed in full evening dress with white bow-ties and long-tailed coats, speaking in snooty voices: "Boys! Come here, boys. We only want your blood." One bite from their fangs would drain the blood out of the body of a boy or rabbit.

The boys and rabbit huddled together, trembling with fear. The Venomous Vampires were taking napkins from their pockets (they did not want to splatter blood over their clothes) when from the pond there came a glug, glug, glug.

"Come on, ducky rocky. Come on! Come on! Tell us what to do," cried the boys, as the Venomous Vampires opened their mouths and licked their fangs.

The ducky rocky normally swam to the surface once or twice a day. He was almost exhausted. He reached the surface, gasped for air, cried, "Muddy hands!" before sinking once more to the bottom of the pond.

Quickly the boys bent down, stuck their hands in the muddy ground and held them out towards the Venomous Vampires. The Venomous Vampires screamed, "Oh no! Not the muddy hands!" as their heads shot off and bounced away and their bodies ran off to the dry cleaners.

"What luck," gasped the boys wiping their hands on their pullovers.

The boys and rabbit were still trembling when from between the trees there appeared Scary Scots dressed in kilts and playing bagpipes. The boys and rabbit screamed in horror. Globerous Ghosts are bad, Mystic Mummies very bad, Venomous Vampires very, very bad, but Scary Scots with bagpipes are even worse. Five minutes of that sound and a boy (or rabbit) will explode.

The five minutes were almost up when from the pond there came a glug, glug, glug.

"Come on, ducky rocky. Come on! Come on! Tell us what to do," cried the boys, as the bagpipes wheezed and groaned and filled their ears with deadly sound.

The ducky rocky swam as hard as he could, reached the surface but, before he could speak, sank to the bottom: he was exhausted. "We've had it," cried the boys and rabbit in despair.

But at that moment two Hero Hedgehogs ran out of the bushes (they should have been Horrid Hedgehogs but the spell had gone wrong). They saluted smartly, and stuck their bottoms in the air facing the Scary Scots.

With very rude sounds, spines shot out of their bottoms. The spines punctured the bagpipes sending Scary Scots all over the forest like burst balloons. The boys and Scrooey-Looey cheered and cheered.

The Hero Hedgehogs got up and saluted smartly. They had run out of ammunition: their bottoms were bare. They ran off into the forest to reload.

As soon as they had disappeared, a flapping noise filled the air. The boys looked up in despair as huge butterflies with sickly pink wings flew down upon them.

The Bilious Butterflies seized the boys and rabbit and carried them struggling to a gnarled old man in a glade in the middle of the forest.

IV

The Bilious Butterflies dropped the boys and rabbit at the feet of the gnarled old man. He was very angry. "You have destroyed my pets," he snarled. "My Globerous Ghosts are in globs all over the forest; my Mystic Mummies have unravelled; the heads of my Venomous Vampires are bouncing around like footballs - their bodies have gone to the dry cleaners; my Scary Scots are stuck at the top of trees."

"Hip, hip, hooray!" cried the boys.

"Quiet!" screamed the gnarled old man. "You will not escape. You will become my pets." The boys and rabbit quaked with fear. "Now let me see. I am up to Z. You will be Zany Zombies."

"What are Zany Zombies?" asked the boys in dread.

"The living dead. They have faces of green and purple stripes. Quite attractive if you like that sort of thing."

The boys and Scrooey-Looey did not. "Couldn't we stay as we are?"

"Definitely not."

As the gnarled old man turned away and reached for his magic staff he did not notice four Precious Plants (they should have been Putrid Plants but the spell had gone wrong) creep up behind the boys and rabbit and jump into their pockets.

The gnarled old man gave an evil laugh. "I shall enjoy having Zany Zombies creeping through the forest. They will add a little colour."

He pointed his magic staff at the boys and rabbit and uttered a curse but the little plants reversed the magic: the gnarled old man became a Zany Zombie and with a scream of fury disappeared into the forest to find the antidote.

"That was a bit of luck," sighed the boys. "If only we could get out of this forest."

At that moment four Racing Racoons came to the rescue (they should have been Rancid Racoons but the spell had gone wrong). They rode motorbikes through the forest, revving the engines hard, speeding between the trees.

"Get up behind us," they cried. "Once we were boys like you. We hate that cruel old man. We are here to rescue you."

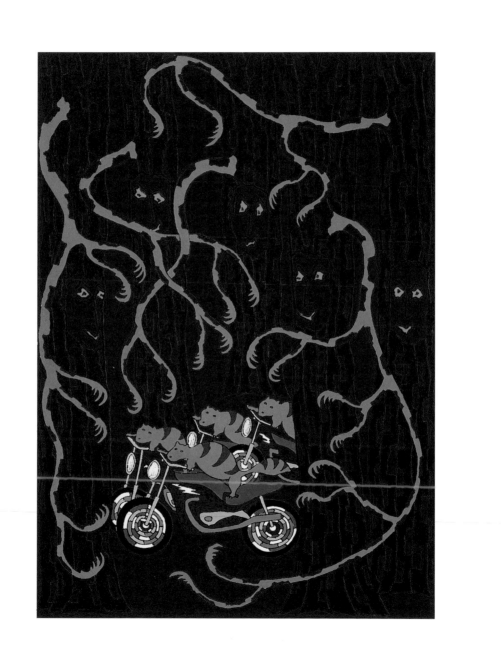

They sped between the trunks of the trees, which tried to bend down to catch the boys but were too stiff and slow. The Racing Racoons left their passengers just outside the forest and roared off.

The boys and Scrooey-Looey lay down in the grass. Scrooey-Looey wiped a paw across his brow and moaned, "I have a slight headache. I led a fairly quiet life before I met you lot."

V

Goblins pounced with spears and net. They threw Scrooey-Looey into a nearby bush, chained the boys in the back of their van and drove to the market.

"Lot Number 55," cried the Head Goblin who was in charge of the auction. "Boys. Three boys. Almost new. Mint condition. Going cheap."

The boys were on the platform with the other merchandise. Anxiously they strained their necks to see who would bid for them. In the back row was a fat lady, Miss Poggenpop, with her friend, Miss Clack. They were cooks at the castle who needed boys to do the washing up. In front of them was a fat man with a rhino whip, wanting slaves for his plantation. The bidding was fierce.

"£5. Will anyone give me £5?" Miss Poggenpop raised her stick. "£10?" The fat man cracked his whip. "£15?" Miss Poggenpop raised her stick. "£20?" The fat man cracked his whip. "£25?" Miss Poggenpop shook her head.

"Oh no," sighed the boys. "The fat man's going to get us." Then a voice at the back squeaked, "£25!" "£25. Will anyone give me £30?" The fat man shook his head. "Going, going, gone. Sold to the rabbit for £25."

Scrooey-Looey ran forward and handed over the money. The boys were free. They ran outside. "Thank you, Scrooey-Looey! But where did you get the money?" The rabbit yawned. He had been up all night in the lettuce bar: "Oh, just a few games of cards."

But then a loud voice boomed: "How nice to see you, boys. Do join me for supper." It was Griselda. "Oh no!" they cried.

"Oh yes!" drooled Griselda. "This time I shall bind you up straight away." She pointed her magic staff at them, uttered a spell and heavy balls of iron, chains and rope flew through the air. "Got you! Got you! Got you!" cried Griselda.

But the little plants were still in their pockets and quickly reversed the magic. Balls and chains snapped shut around Griselda's wrists. She staggered under the weight. Rope wound up and down her body and round her ankles.

Scrooey-Looey picked up the end of the rope, and pulled it hard. Griselda swayed, tottered and fell with a splash into a puddle. She would have screamed, but a gag sprang across her mouth. "Mmmmm!" she mumbled, struggling uselessly.

At that moment Snuggle arrived. The cat was back from a hunting trip and had come to rescue the boys and rabbit. "Snuggle!" they cried. "We are pleased to see you." "We've had enough of this adventure." "We've met all sorts of dreadful creatures." "Can you take us home?"

"But of course," said the cat, giving a sudden roar and turning into a lion. He grew a pair of golden wings. "Get on my back."

They flew towards the Garden. The boys and rabbit laughed and sang. It was wonderful to be alive. Snuggle landed beside an open door in a high brick wall.

"Follow us," squeaked the Precious Plants, as they jumped out of the pockets and led the way into the Garden.

"Welcome! Welcome!" cried the Gardener. "You are just in time for supper. Then you must get home before you are missed."